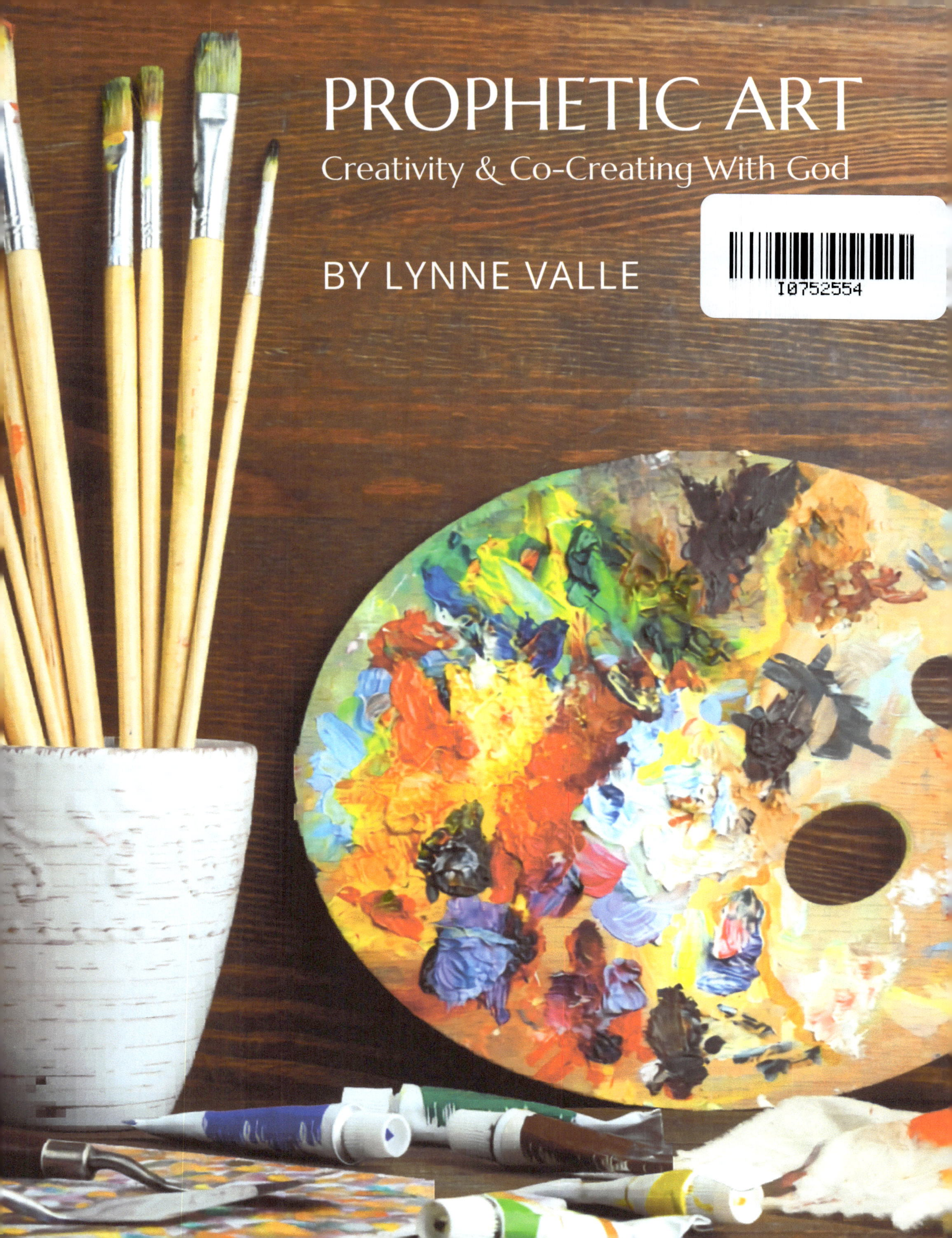
PROPHETIC ART
Creativity & Co-Creating With God
BY LYNNE VALLE

Prophetic Art: Creativity & Co-Creating With God

Lenexa, KS USA
lynnevalle.shop
gloryrain.store
lynnevalle.com

All bold Scripture quotations were added by the author for emphasis.

Library of Congress Control Number: 2026901061
ISBN: (paperback) 979-8-9992068-5-5

This book contains the opinions and ideas of the author. It serves solely informational and educational purposes and should not replace professional medical care, mental health care, financial advice, or any other professional services. This book's author and publisher accept no responsibility for losses resulting from its content.

Printed in the United States of America
First edition 2026.

ACKNOWLEDGEMENTS

With sincere gratitude, I thank Kirsty Pennington for generously allowing the inclusion of her beautiful painting, A New Hope.

Books By Lynne Valle

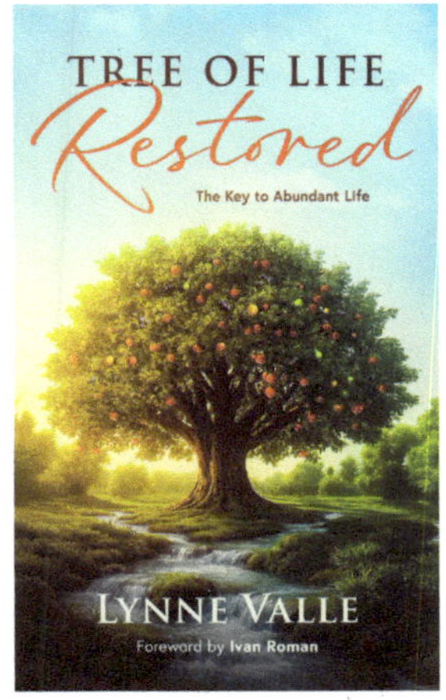

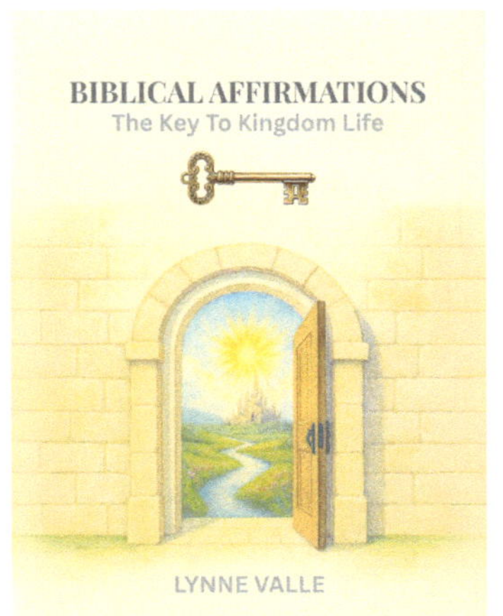

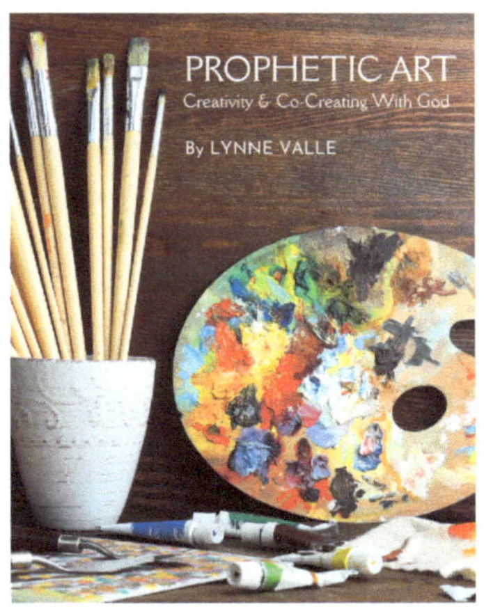

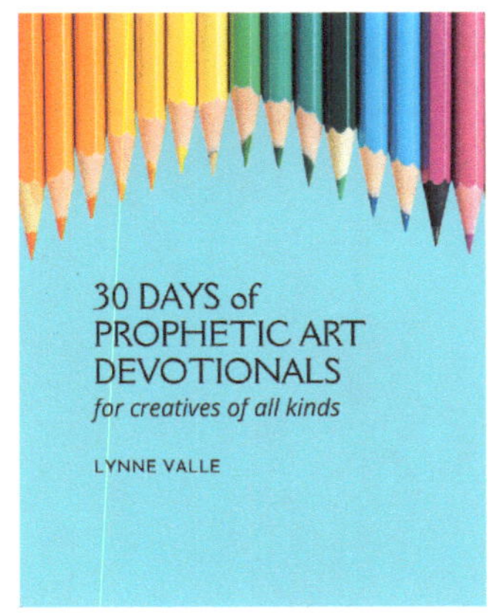

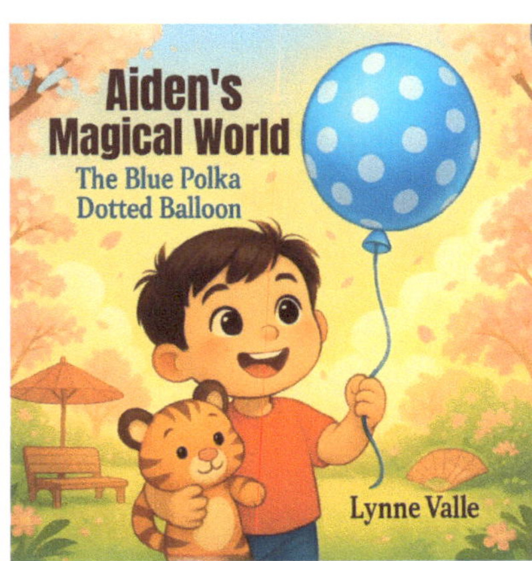

www.lynnevalle.shop

www.lynnevalle.com

Table of Contents

Introduction

Welcome to a journey of creativity, freedom, and divine partnership. This book is an invitation to enter into the radical good news of the New Covenant, a place where creativity is not just a human gift but a powerful expression of God's heart revealed through us. Prophetic art is more than paint on canvas or music in the air—it's where Heaven meets earth, a living demonstration of who God is and how deeply He desires to collaborate with us.

In the New Covenant, we live not under the shadow of law or performance, but in the radiant presence of Christ's finished work. Creativity is no longer a striving for approval or a way to earn love. Instead, it is response to a lavish grace, a yielded partnership with the Holy Spirit. You were born to create, and you were destined to do it with God, not just for Him.

This is radically good news—especially for those who have felt limited, disqualified, or uncertain in their creative journey. You are not alone or left to figure it out. Through the Holy Spirit, God invites every believer into a life where creativity flourishes, prophecies are tangible, and art becomes an expression—both personal and prophetic—of His love.

Get ready to discover a relationship that changes everything. Through this book, you'll encounter stories, teaching, and practical insights that will inspire you to step into your new covenant identity as a creative being, fully alive in partnership with God.

"

We are engineered by his design; he molded and manufactured us in Christ. We are his workmanship, his poetry. We are fully fit to do good, equipped to give attractive evidence of his likeness in us in everything we do.

Ephesians 2:10 (THE MIRROR)

New Covenant Creativity—A Fresh Perspective

"Fullness of joy" means high-voltage, lightning-bolt joy that makes you want to wriggle out of your skin every single second from the extreme ectasy and bliss of His presence!"

Georgian Banov

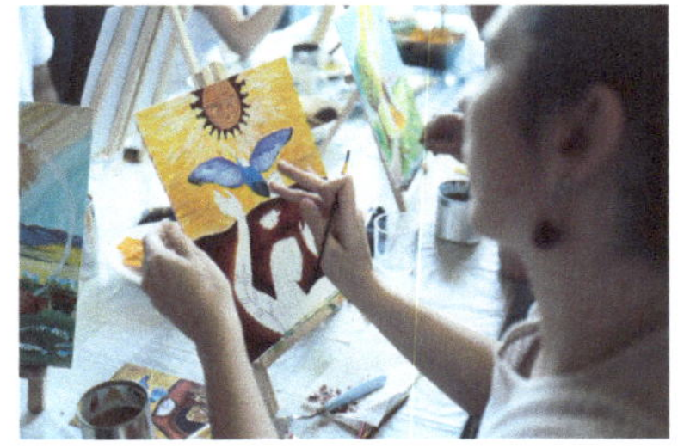

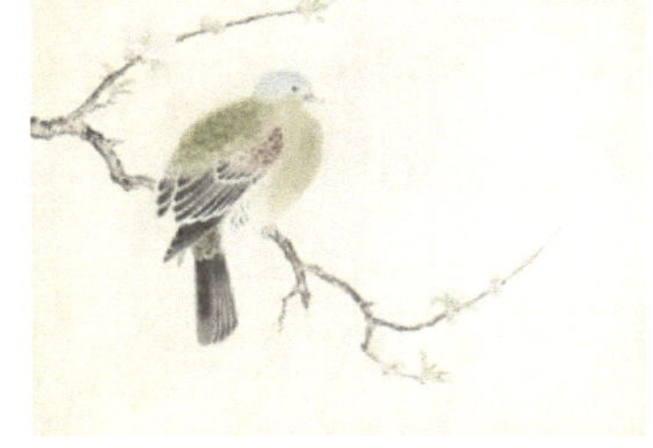

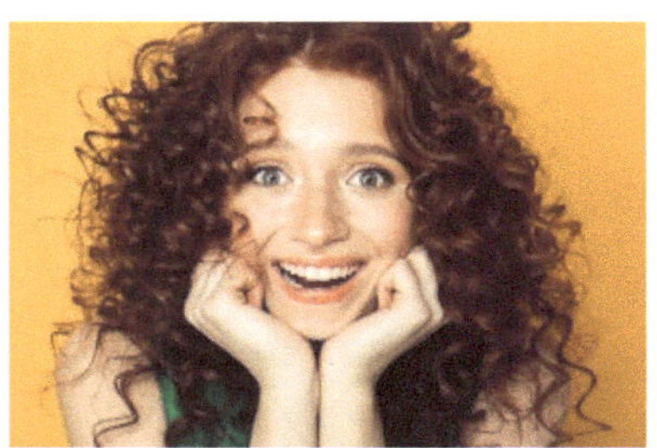

Freedom for Expression

The New Covenant doesn't just lift burdens; it unleashes creative expression. You are designed to reflect God's nature, and creativity is a part of that divine DNA. In Christ, fear, shame, and performance melt away—freedom for authentic self-expression is restored.

Creativity as Relationship

You are not called to create alone. The Holy Spirit is the great inspirer. Prophetic art reveals that creativity is about relationship—God speaking, you responding, together releasing beauty that changes hearts.

Joy as Your Permission Slip

One of the greatest fruits of new covenant creativity is joy—a true sense of delight in God's presence. When you create with God, you are free to enjoy the process, not just the product. Joy becomes your permission slip to keep going and growing.

What is Prophetic Art? Redefining Creativity with God

Prophetic art is the practice of creating art in partnership with the Holy Spirit, listening for God's heart, and translating what He reveals into visual, musical, or written expression. Unlike secular creativity, which often centers around personal vision or emotion, prophetic art is fueled by intimacy with God and a desire to convey His message to others.

A key aspect of prophetic art is learning to recognize and trust the voice of God as He speaks uniquely to you and through you. Prophetic creativity flows from intimacy—hearing His whisper, sensing His guidance, and allowing His heart to shape what you create. As you lean into your God-given design and purpose, you become a vessel for His expression on the earth, releasing what only you can carry. Through this holy partnership, your art becomes more than skill or inspiration—it becomes a living conversation between Heaven and earth.

Prophetic art is not limited to painting. It can include music, writing, dance, sculpture—any creative medium where the artist responds to the Spirit's prompting. Every believer is invited into this way of creating. You do not need to be a professional, trained, or even experienced to begin. What matters is a willingness to listen, trust, and respond.

Sadly, many have believed that creativity is only for a select few. This restricted mindset keeps people from experiencing the joy and transformation of prophetic art. But the New Covenant breaks those limitations. God, the ultimate Creator, has made you in His image, and His Spirit dwells in you. As you create prophetically, you are aligning with the Creator's intent—drawing heaven's reality to earth.

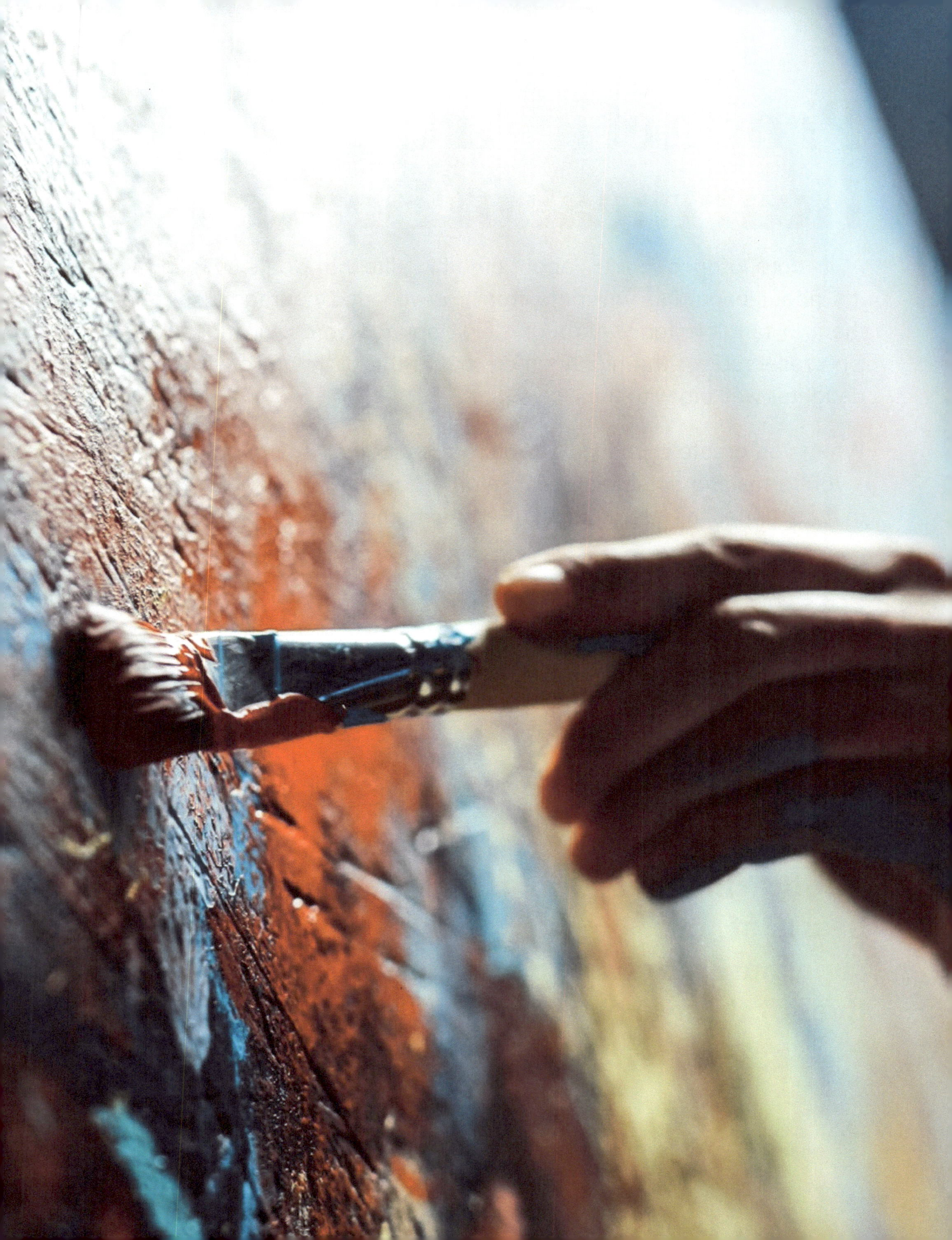

Prophetic Art: The Heartbeat of Heaven

At its core, prophetic art is about breathing life into God's unseen realities. It's about capturing whispers from Heaven and courageously releasing them in tangible form—through color, sound, words, or movement. This isn't reserved for the highly gifted, but is the birthright of every son and daughter walking with the Holy Spirit.

When you create prphetically, you're not just making something beautiful - you're making something alive. You are releasing a spiritual resonance that continues ministering long after the moment of creation.

Each act of prophetic creativity becomes a conversation, a statement that God's voice is not distant but active, personal, and loving. When you say yes to prophetic art, you become a vessel—the brushstroke of God's affection on the earth, releasing healing, encouragement, and hope.

Prophetic art forms a bridge - between Heaven and earth, between God's heart and your own heart. And as you co-create with Him, you step into your original design: a beloved son or daughter who reflects the beauty, power, and goodness of your Creator.

"Embracing our design, which originated in the heart of our creator, gives us the freedom to supernaturally use that creativity to transform the lives of those around us."

Theresa Dedmon

Prophetic Art Forms

Prophetic art takes many forms—sometimes it emerges as a painting created in the middle of worship, where every stroke feels like a response to His presence. Other times it comes as a spontaneous melody that rises from the heart without warning, carrying the sound of Heaven in a way words could never fully express. Each expression is a sacred moment of co-creating with God.

It can also look like a poem birthed in quiet prayer, where simple phrases suddenly carry weight, revelation, and tenderness. Prophetic creativity doesn't have to be loud or dramatic; it often comes softly, unexpectedly, in the places where your heart is turned toward Him. What you create in those moments becomes a reflection of the dialogue happening between your spirit and His.

The diversity of prophetic art is endless because the Spirit has infinite ways to reveal God's heart. He moves through color, sound, movement, story, and symbol in ways that are deeply personal and wonderfully diverse. No two prophetic expressions are the same, because no two journeys with God are the same. And in that beautiful variety, His voice is made known again and again.

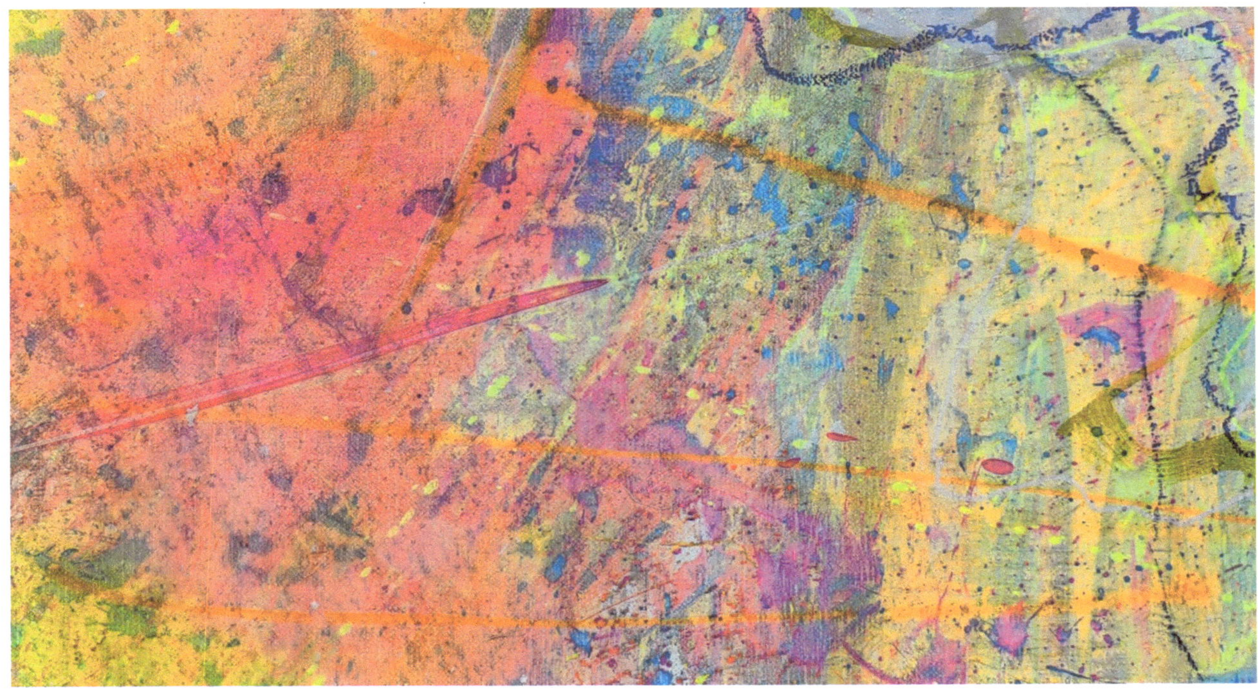

Creating is Worship

Every act of prophetic creativity is worship. It's a response to the awe-inspiring beauty of God and an offering that invites others to encounter Him in new ways. Create from a posture of honor, joy, and wonder.

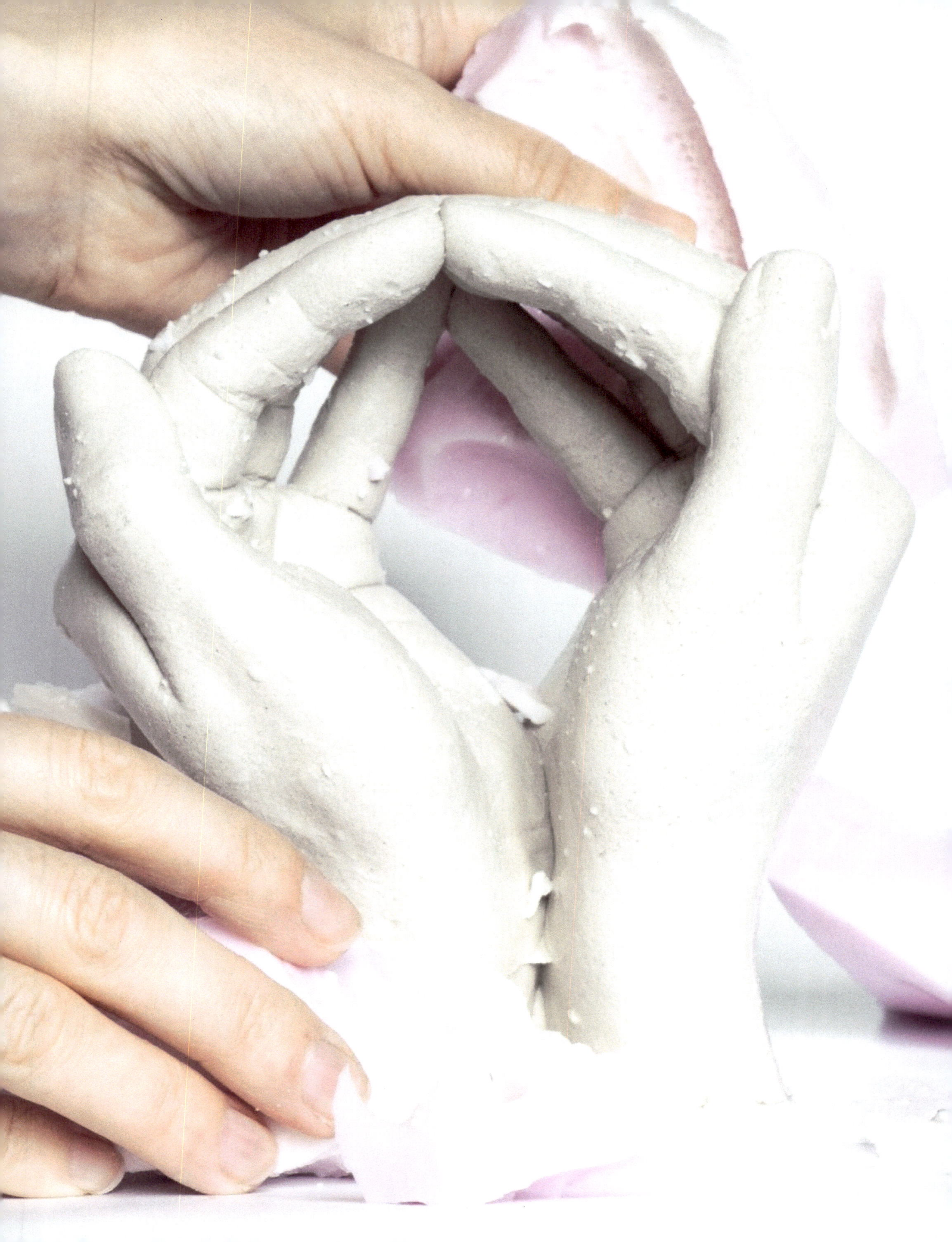

The Holy Spirit: Source, Guide, & Empowerment

The Holy Spirit is not only the giver of creative gifts but the very source, guide, and empowering presence behind prophetic art. When Jesus promised the Spirit, He promised a new kind of relationship—one where creative inspiration and divine direction would flow together seamlessly. The Spirit doesn't just give you a vision and leave; He walks with you in the creative process, whispering ideas, providing insight, and giving courage to step out.

In prophetic art, when you step into the flow of the Holy Spirit, God has a way of opening doors that you could never force open on your own. As you create from a place of obedience and intimacy, He orchestrates divine appointments with the right people at the right time—individuals who recognize, affirm, or are impacted by the anointing on your creative expression. In that flow, supernatural favor begins to surround your work, guiding it farther than your natural resources or connections ever could. God breathes on what you create, positioning it—and you—exactly where His purpose intends.

In prophetic art, the Holy Spirit often surprises us. He births new themes, brings fresh revelation, and sometimes even uses our creative mistakes to uncover deeper truths. Learning to rely on His empowerment means letting go of the need to control results or impress others. Instead, you discover a flow—creativity that is alive, transformative, and rooted in relational trust.

Ask Him questions. Listen for His voice in colors, symbols, melodies, or words. Trust that He delights to create with you. Every believer is invited to practice, to grow, and to explore prophetic creativity in the safety and kindness of the Holy Spirit's companionship.

Then he said, "This is God's message to Zerubbabel: 'Not by might, nor by power, but by my Spirit, says the Lord Almighty—you will succeed because of my Spirit."

Zachariah 4:6 (TPT)

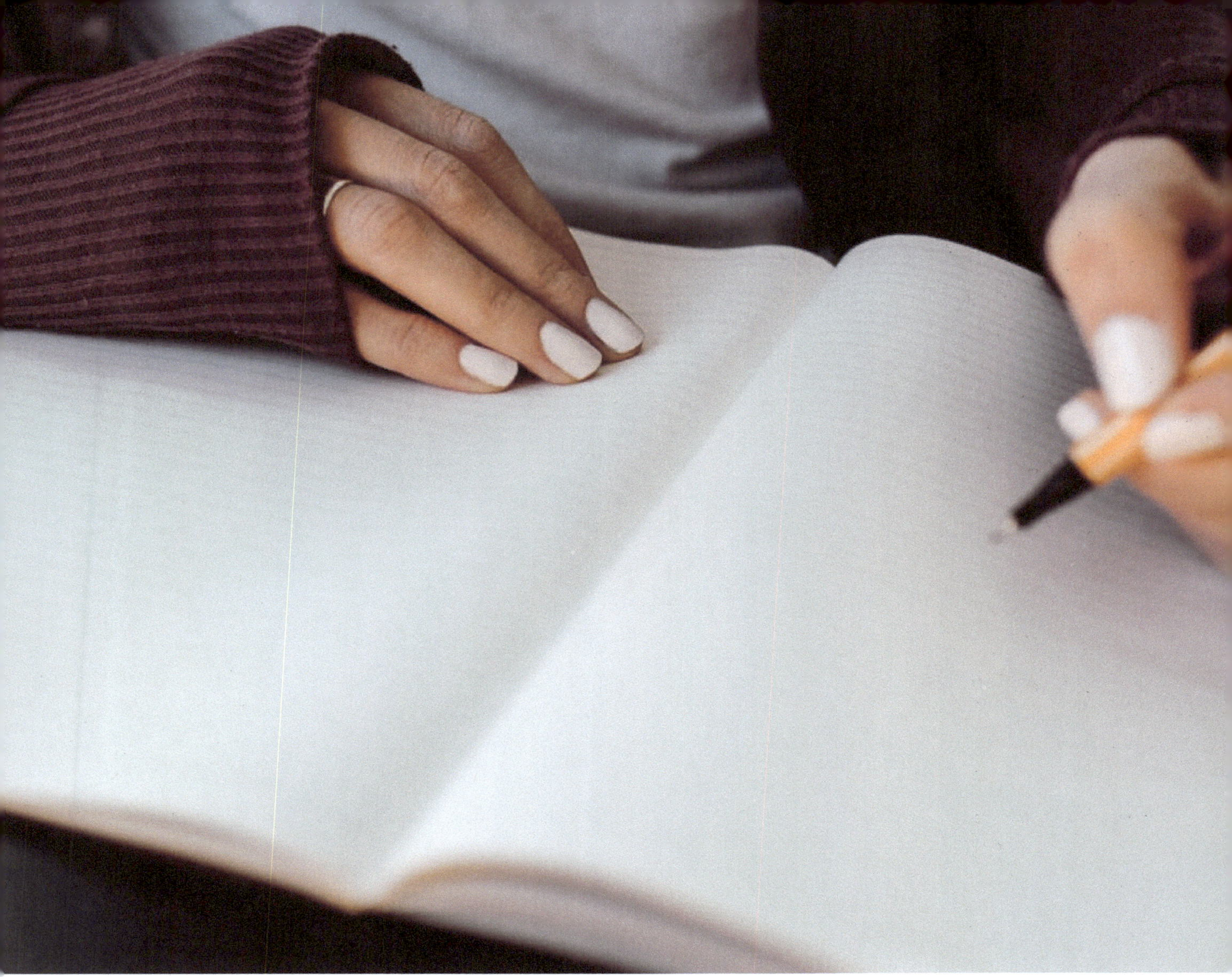

"

I promise you this - the Holy Spirit will come upon you and you will be seized with power.

Jesus Christ, Acts 1:8 , (TPT)

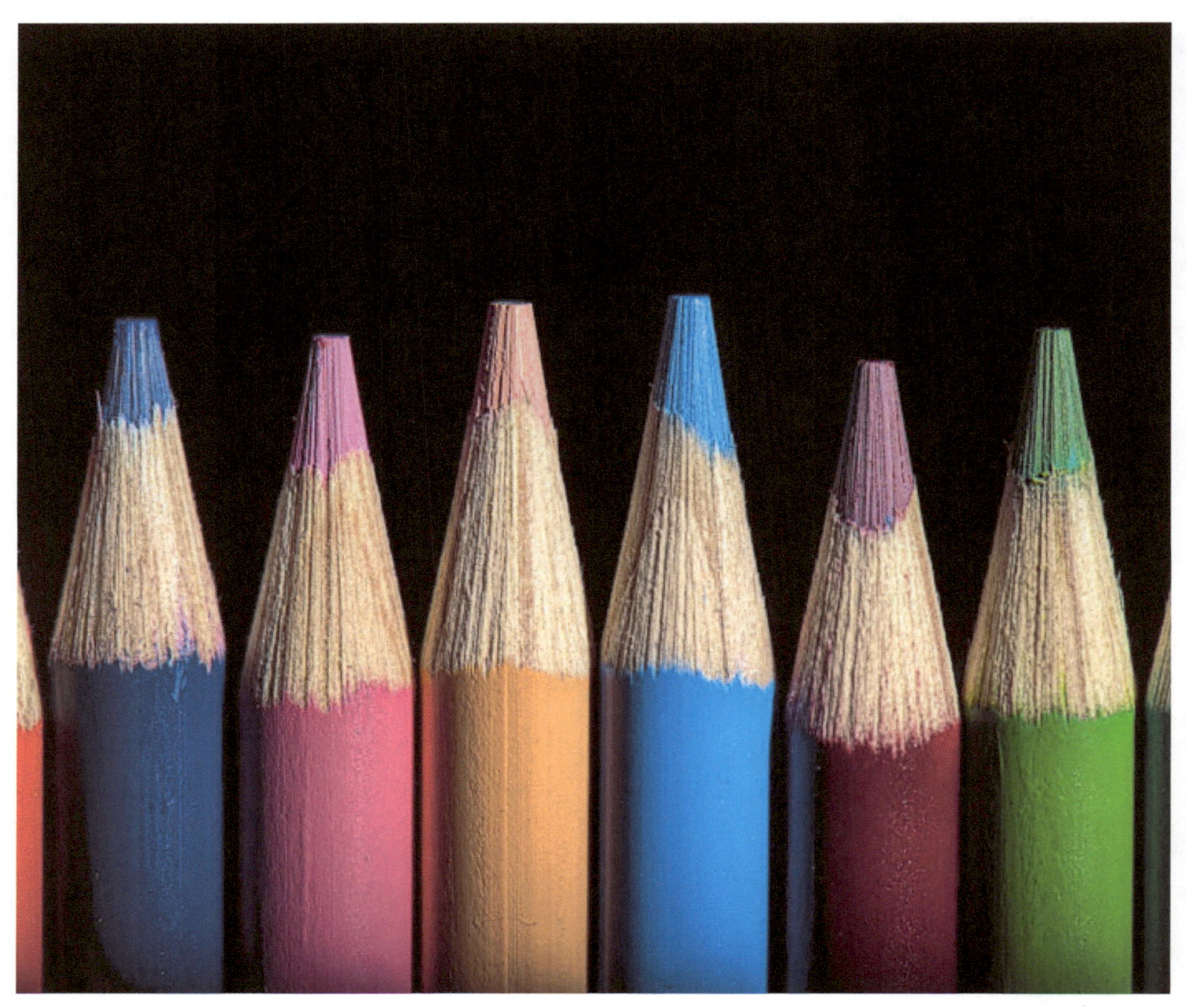

"

Prophetic art is creating with God for the purpose of transforming those that see it and create it. It's a beutiful dance where we as artists cooperate with the Holy Spirit.

Matt Tommey

Fresh Inspiration

The Holy Spirit inspires beyond our natural abilities. When you yield your art or music to Him, He can infuse it with meaning that surpasses skill or technique. Trust that the source of creativity is supernatural—He loves to surprise you with new ideas. In His presence, fresh revelation begins to flow, releasing colors, phrases, melodies, and images you never would have imagined on your own. He awakens new dimensions of creativity within you, stretching your vision and expanding your artistic language. As you stay sensitive to His leading, He continually refreshes your imagination, breathing life into every act of prophetic expression.

Guidance in the Process

From the inception of an idea to its completion, the Spirit guides as a gentle teacher. He breathes direction into every stage of the creative process—sometimes giving you clear vision, other times inviting you to step forward in faith without knowing the full picture. Sometimes He nudges you to pause, to rest, or to take a bold risk that stretches you beyond your comfort zone. As you create, He highlights details, shifts your perspective, and reveals layers of meaning you didn't see at first. Learning to recognize and follow His leading transforms your artistic journey from striving into abiding, where every brushstroke, lyric, or movement becomes an act of partnership with Him.

Empowerment for Impact

Prophetic art empowered by the Spirit carries an authority and impact that transforms lives. When the Holy Spirit breathes on what you create, it becomes more than beauty—it becomes a conduit of His presence. He empowers us to release healing, hope, breakthrough, and encouragement, often speaking directly to the hearts of people in ways words alone never could. Prophetic art becomes a vessel of ministry wherever it is received, carrying the power to shift atmospheres, awaken identity, and reveal the heart of God with clarity and tenderness. In His hands, your creativity becomes a weapon of light and a wellspring of life.

Partnering with God: Hearing & Responding Creatively

The adventure of prophetic art starts with God's voice and ends with a creative response. Partnership with God is not a one-sided conversation. It is alive, interactive, and often playful. Sometimes the ideas come clearly in a moment. Other times, listening to God in the creative process is slow, unfolding bit by bit as you trust Him.

The key is learning to recognize the gentle promptings of the Holy Spirit. These can arrive as visions, mental images, words, impressions, or even deep emotions. Once you receive something, respond in faith—putting brush to canvas, fingers to keyboard, or melody in the air. Don't worry about perfection; God honors the heart behind your response.

In this partnership, you discover that God's creativity is not limited by your skill level or experience. The ultimate goal is connection—creating something together with the Lord that reveals His love, beauty, and encouragement not only to you but to the world around you.

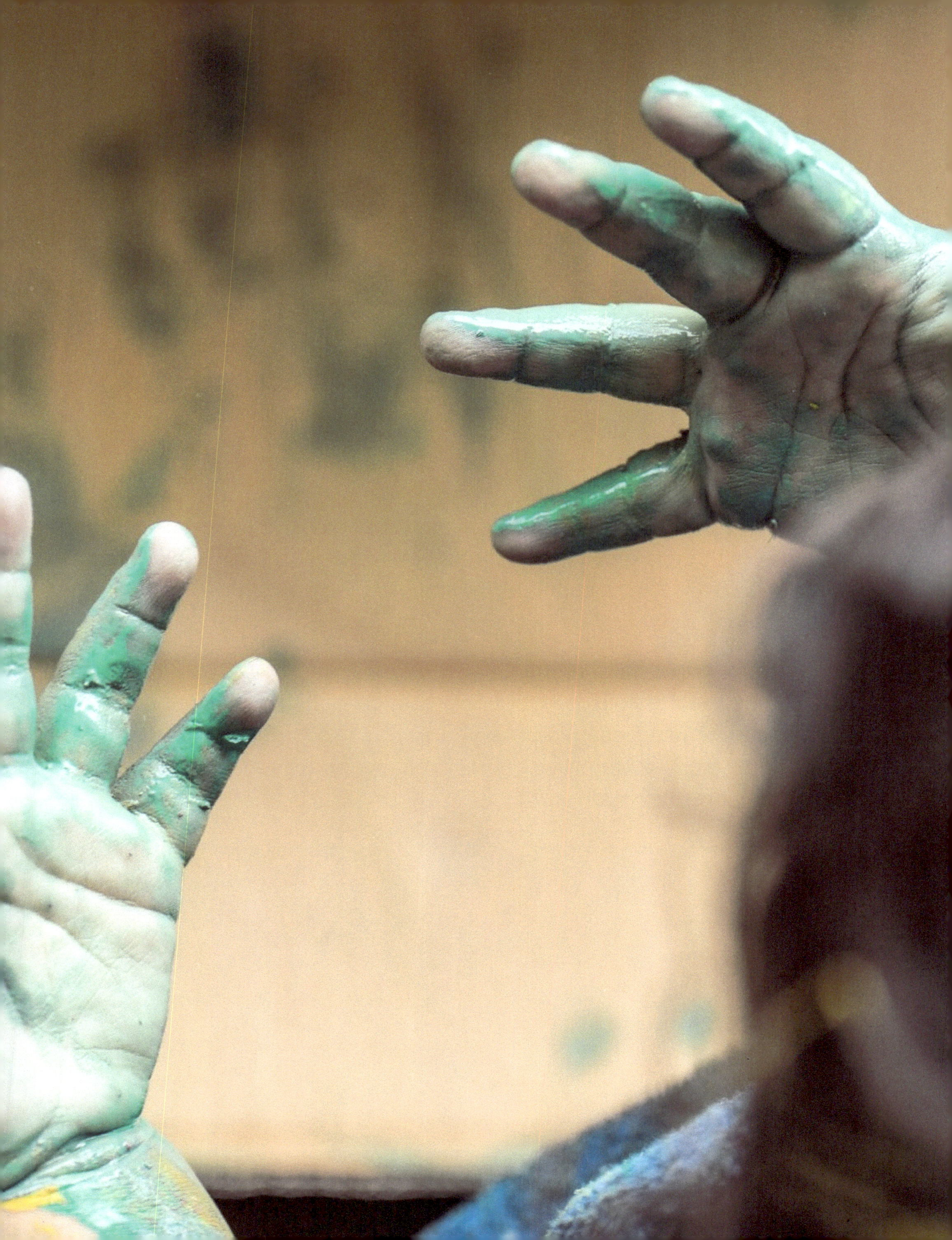

Living 100% Led by the Spirit

One of the joys of prophetic art is discovering how God delights in every detail of your creative journey. Being 100% led by the Spirit means letting Him direct not just the art you make but the way you see yourself as a creative person. Testimonies from artists worldwide show how God moves when we surrender control and trust His leading.

For some, the Spirit's guidance comes as a gentle nudge to paint a particular image during worship for someone specific. For others, it's an unexplainable urge to step out and release a song they've never sung before. In both cases, powerful stories emerge—hearts are healed, minds are renewed, and communities are encouraged through these acts of obedience and boldness.

The practical outworking of being Spirit-led is trust. Trust that God is a far better guide than fear. Trust that His presence is with you whether you're experienced or just beginning. As you say yes to Him, you'll find stories multiplying—stories that prove you can live every day led and empowered by the Spirit in your creative practice.

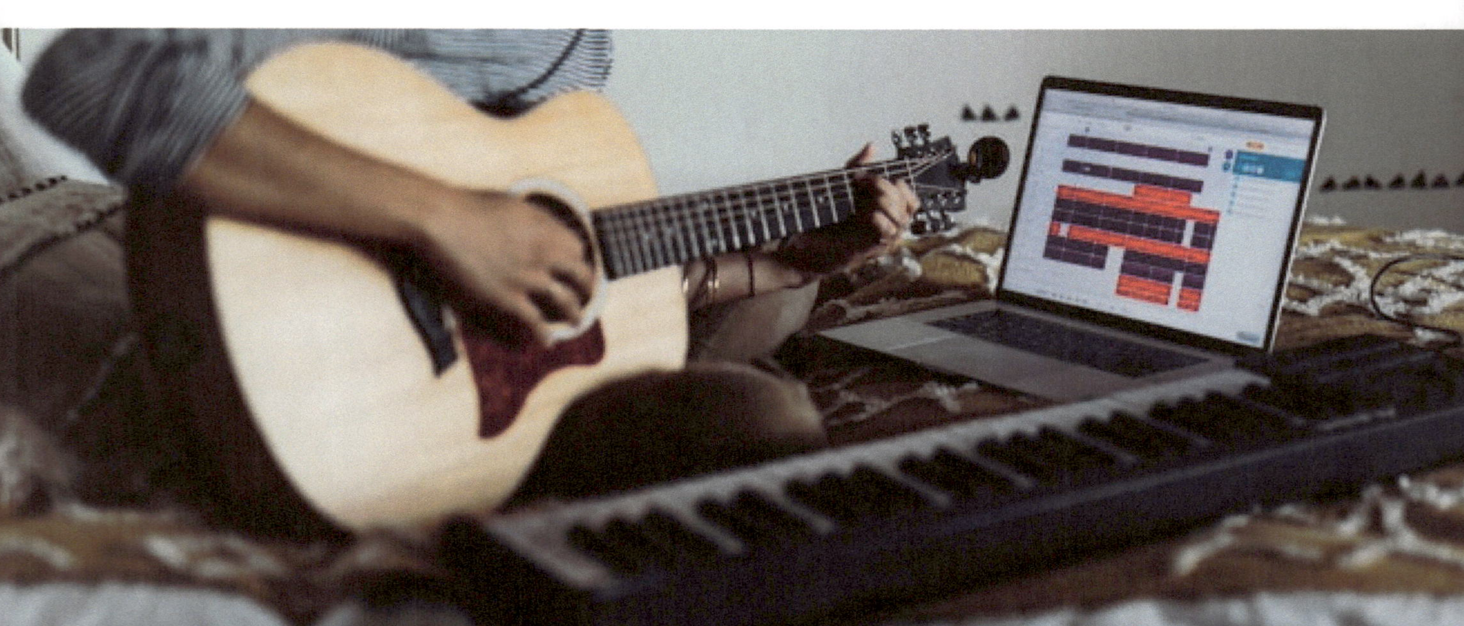

Listening in Love

God speaks in unique and tender ways to each of us. Whether through mental pictures, dreams, song lyrics, or subtle impressions—He loves to initiate creative conversations. Take time to quiet your mind and simply listen. Love, not performance, is the atmosphere that empowers creative response.

Responding in Faith

Responding to inspiration from the Holy Spirit doesn't require understanding every detail. Sometimes, just taking the first step opens the door for more revelation. Obedience in small things leads to greater confidence and clarity as you move forward creatively.

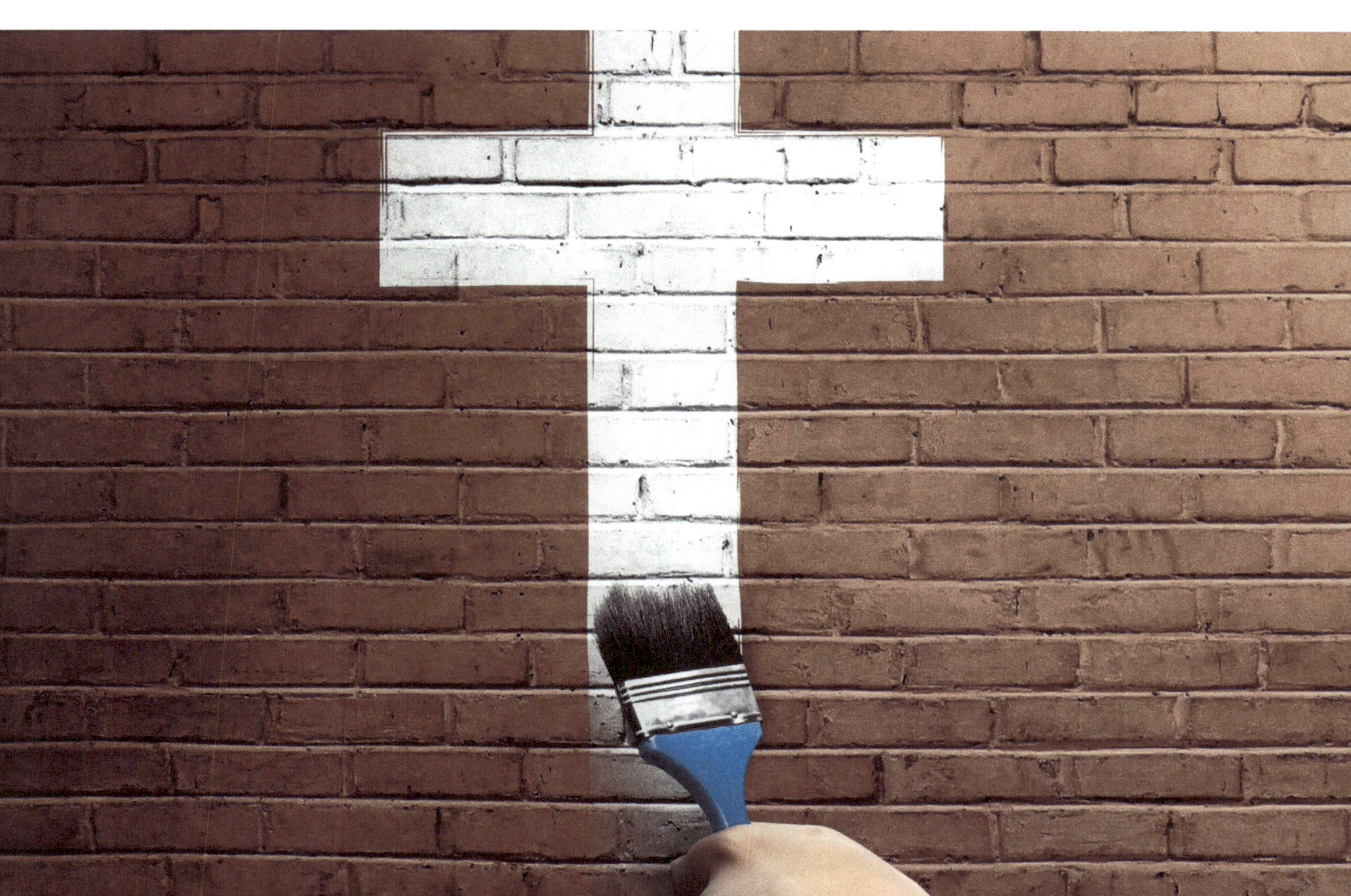

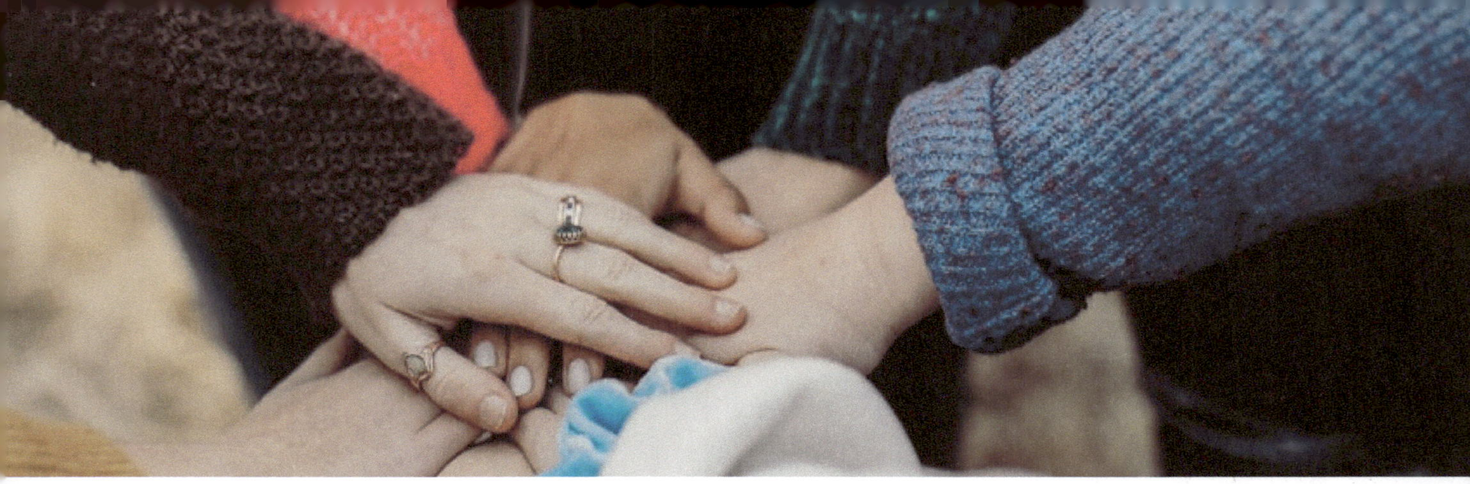

Healing Stories

Time and again, prophetic artists testify to the healing power of creative acts led by the Spirit. Paintings, songs, or dances have brought physical, emotional, and spiritual breakthrough—demonstrating God's kindness in supernatural ways.

Transformation Through Obedience

Every act of obedience, whether big or small, is part of a larger story God is writing. Testimonies reveal that stepping out in faith releases transformation not just to others but to the artists themselves, creating new boldness and joy.

Community Encouragement

Prophetic art, when shared, strengthens communities. Whether through congregational worship paintings or mural projects, God often uses creativity to unify, encourage, and remind people of their shared identity in Christ.

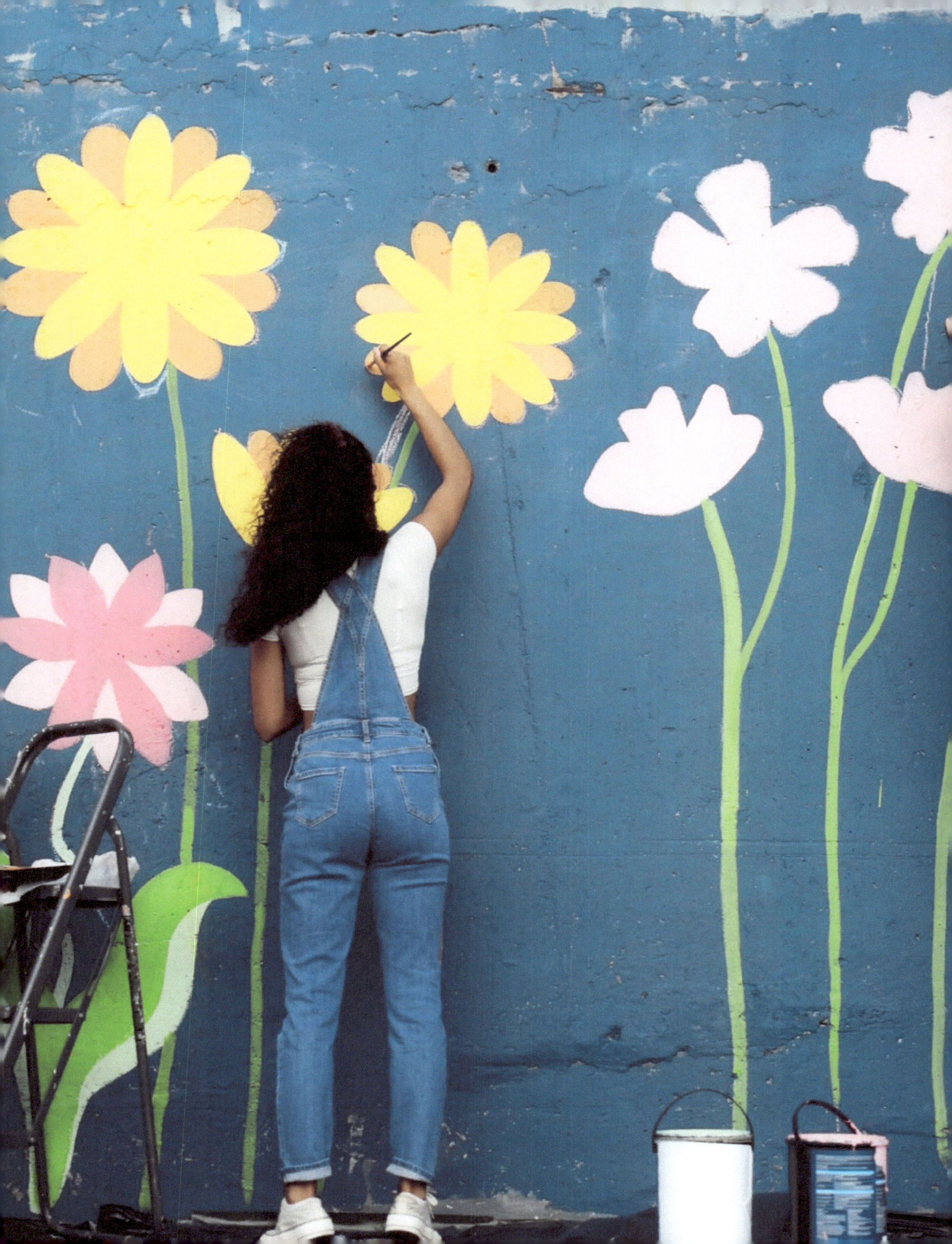

My Testimony: Wrapped in Glory, Met by Opposition

One Sunday at church, I was being ministered to by a prophetic, anointed minister. He released a beautiful prophetic word over me, and I had an amazing encounter with the Holy Spirit. I was still basking in that glory when I stepped into the public area at the back of the chapel. Suddenly, a church leader approached me with a spirit of rage. I was absolutely shocked by her behavior. She raised her voice, made false accusations, and aggressively confronted me—her main issue being her disagreement with the teaching in my book. She was verbally abusive, would not let me say a single word, and then turned her back and walked away.

The shift was so jarring. One moment I was wrapped in the presence of the Spirit, and the next I felt spiritually and verbally assaulted. I admit, I was very upset. My book represents years of hard work, prayer, and research—something I poured my heart into. Her attack wasn't just against me; it felt like an attack on my ministry and my calling.

The Shock of the Shift

In sacred spaces, contrasts can be stark. Joy to grief, affirmation to accusation, silence to shouting. The suddenness can leave the soul gasping, as if the atmosphere has been pulled from the room. That is how it felt as I crossed the invisible threshold from the sanctuary's sweetness into the cacophony of contention. The encounter did not merely touch the surface of my emotions; it pressed against the tender places of identity and assignment—the places I had surrendered to God through years of obedience.

Even in that moment of shock, I held to a quiet truth: the same Spirit who had just ministered peace to me had not moved or diminished. His nearness is not subject to the volume of accusation. Yet I am human, and I felt the sting. My book carries the weight of prayer, of nights spent listening, of study and devotion. To have it dismissed with hostility felt like a strike against the very call I cherish. Still, somewhere beneath the swirl, there was a seed of assurance that God would not let this moment define the day.

"

Jesus, Paul and believers throughout the ages faced their greatest opposition from those who knew the Scriptures.

Francois du Toit

A Divine Connection Prepared in Advance

Later that night, as I was scrolling through Facebook, I came across a post by a new Facebook friend, David. He had accepted my friend request only the day before, and I had only sent it because a mutual friend from Kingdom Creative Movement said she felt led to suggest that we connect. I had no idea at the time that God was already arranging a divine appointment—preparing a connection with this lovely couple even before the day's events unfolded.

In David's post was a photograph of a beautiful painting created by his wife, Kirsty Pennington. The image stopped me instantly. It was an exquisite portrait of a woman with pink roses tucked below her hair. As I gazed at the painting, I could feel the confidence, peace, and beauty radiating from the woman in the artwork. There was something so sure, so steady, so unapologetically secure about her expression. And as I continued to look, that's when the shift happened.

The Portrait That Spoke

Art has a way of speaking in a language beyond words, bypassing the mind and ministering directly to the heart. This portrait carried the fragrance of rest. The roses seemed to whisper of tenderness, while the woman's gaze communicated unshakable assurance. It felt as though the painting was not merely an image but an invitation—an echo of heaven's perspective. The contrast to the earlier confrontation was unmistakable: where accusation demanded defense, the painting extended a quiet welcome to simply be—chosen, beloved, called.

As I lingered with the image, I began to sense a sacred exchange. The anxiety of the day lifted its grip, and the weight of the words spoken against me began to dissolve. The Spirit used beauty to interrupt the narrative of attack and to re-anchor my identity. I realized that even before the offense occurred, the Lord had already provided a balm. This was not coincidence; it was orchestration—grace arriving on schedule.

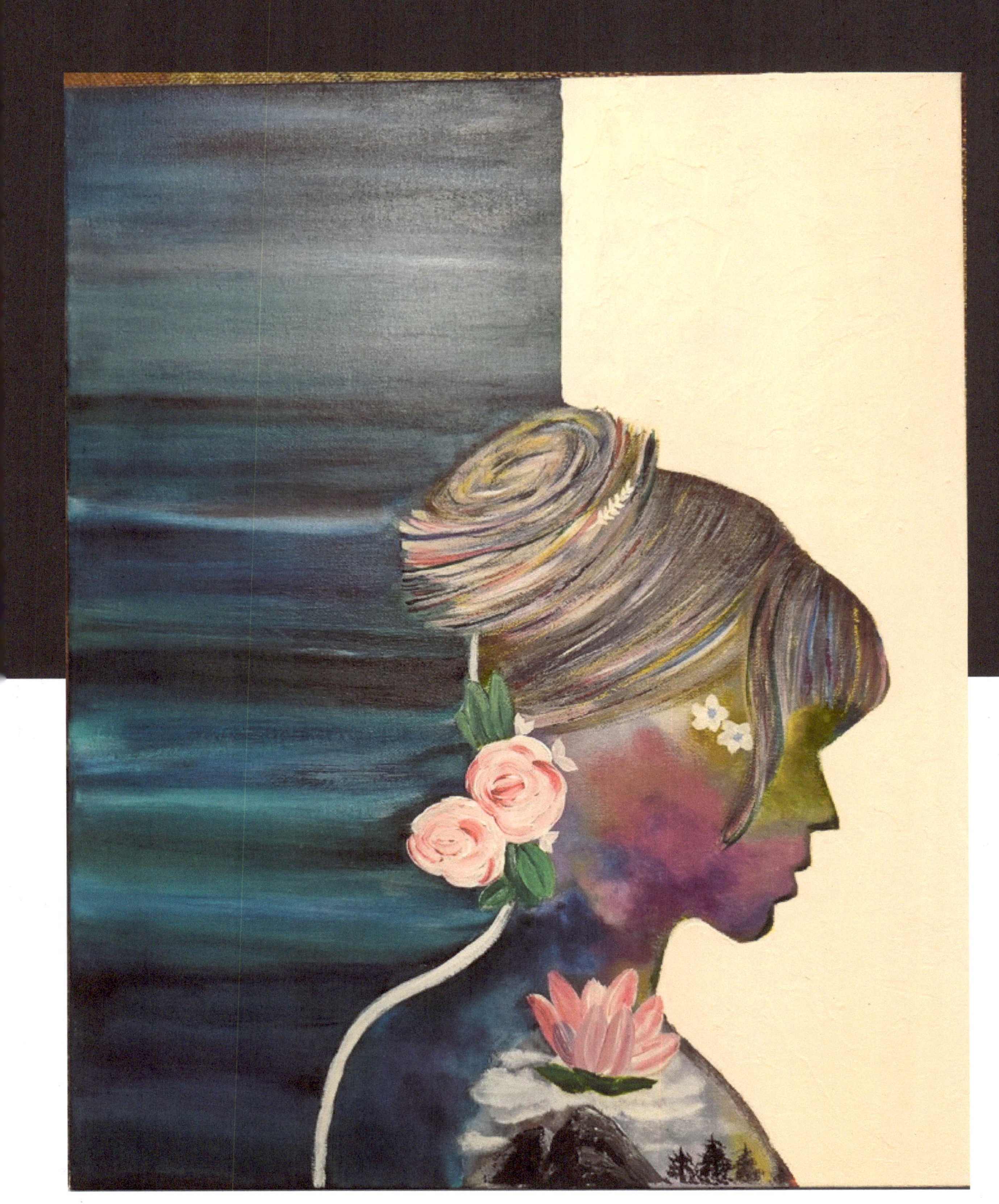

"

I began painting two years ago still trying to find a 'style' but I believe at the moment there is no style. I paint whatever image God plants on my heart and it becomes a burning need to finish until it is done. I paint at home usually while working and parenting so it's great to zone in and just get lost in His presence while we create the image. Usually I get the title during the image, often from revelation about my own walk and life.

For this piece (A New Hope) I really felt like there was a woman leaving behind all of the things that dragged her back, and as I painted I was shown things that I could pray for release from and further healing which would allow me to be free for the things I am stepping into, just like the woman in the painting. If our story can help others then I believe our tools will too, and God showing me deep revelations during the creative process highlights the groups of people that I can then pray for as they see the image, so they can see His love and healing the same way that I do. I then pray over the image before I release it online and pray that the one person who needs to see it and hear from Him will come across it somehow.

Testimony from Prophetic Artist, Kirsty Pennington

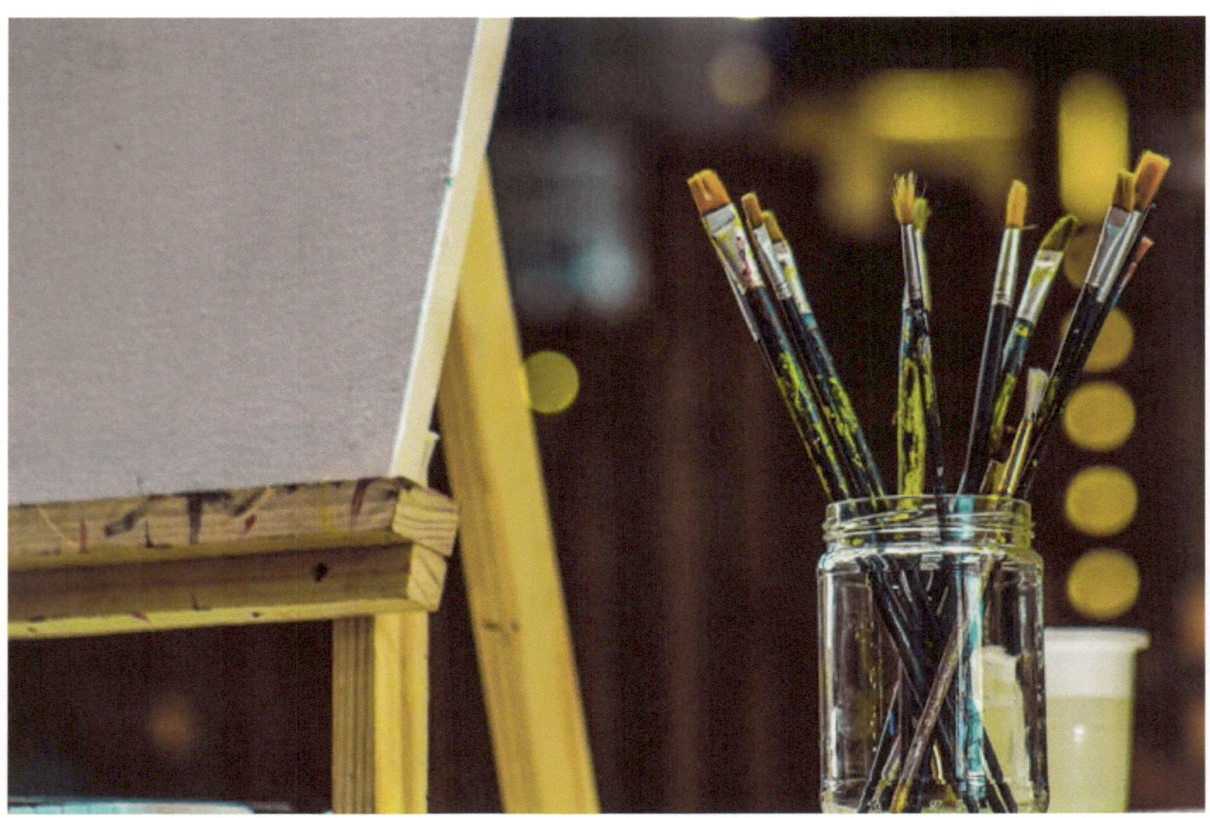

The Whisper: You Are Chosen, You Are Called

Suddenly, I encountered the Holy Spirit in a powerful way. I sensed the Spirit whisper to my heart, "You are chosen. You are called." In that moment, the heaviness I had been carrying from the attack earlier in the day lifted. A deep release washed over me, and a fresh wave of peace, strength, and identity flooded my soul.

What the enemy meant for evil, the Lord had already gone ahead of me to redeem. Even before I knew I would be attacked, God had prepared a moment of healing through a prophetic painting and through a connection with people whose hearts were aligned with His. Instead of being crushed by the enemy's attempt to wound me, I was uplifted, strengthened, and anchored once again in my calling.

Anchored Identity After the Storm

Identity becomes most luminous in contrast with accusation. The Spirit did not rebut each false claim point by point; instead, He reasserted my name and purpose. Chosen. Called. These two words became a canopy over my thoughts, a shelter against the night air of condemnation. Under that canopy, I remembered: my work flows from intimacy, not from striving; my book is an altar of obedience, not a monument to self; my ministry is held by the One who commissioned it. The earlier sting couldn't survive in the warmth of that reminder.

Grace did not erase what happened, but it reframed it. The confrontation became a backdrop against which God's tenderness shone brighter. The painting, the connection with David and Kirsty, and the Spirit's whisper wove together into a testimony: heaven is not reactive; heaven is prepared. And in that preparation, I found courage to keep walking, to keep writing, and to keep releasing what He has placed in my hands.

Rising Above: Holding Peace, Confidence, and Conviction

Unfortunately, the woman who confronted me continued to spread negativity about me and my ministry. But my testimony—my encounter with the Holy Spirit and the prophetic word I received—has become an anchor of peace and strength. It has empowered me to rise above the attacks of the enemy while maintaining my peace, my confidence, and my conviction in who I am in Jesus Christ, and in what He has called me to carry and release.

Attacks may persist, but assignment remains. Peace is not the absence of warfare; it is the presence of the One who commands the seas. Confidence is not arrogance; it is agreement with God's assessment. Conviction is not stubbornness; it is fidelity to the voice that called my name. These truths reoriented my posture. I did not need to chase rumors or rehearse rebuttals. Instead, I chose to steward the testimony I had been given and to keep my hands on the plow of purpose.

A Testimony to Carry Forward

Sometimes the most powerful ministry we offer is not a perfectly argued defense but a quietly consistent life, anchored in encounter. The beauty of that evening–the painting, the providential friendship, the whisper of the Spirit–became a lens through which I saw the day anew. The enemy's attempt to fracture my focus only highlighted the faithfulness of God to restore it. I carry this story now as a gentle banner over my work: chosen and called. Where accusation once tried to write the ending, grace has authored a better chapter.

I rest in the knowledge that God goes before me, prepares connections I cannot foresee, and heals wounds I cannot anticipate. He turns the jarring shifts of life into holy pivots that lead me deeper into peace, courage, and purpose. And so I continue, not because the path is without resistance, but because the One who called me walks beside me–turning every attempt at harm into an opportunity for redemption.

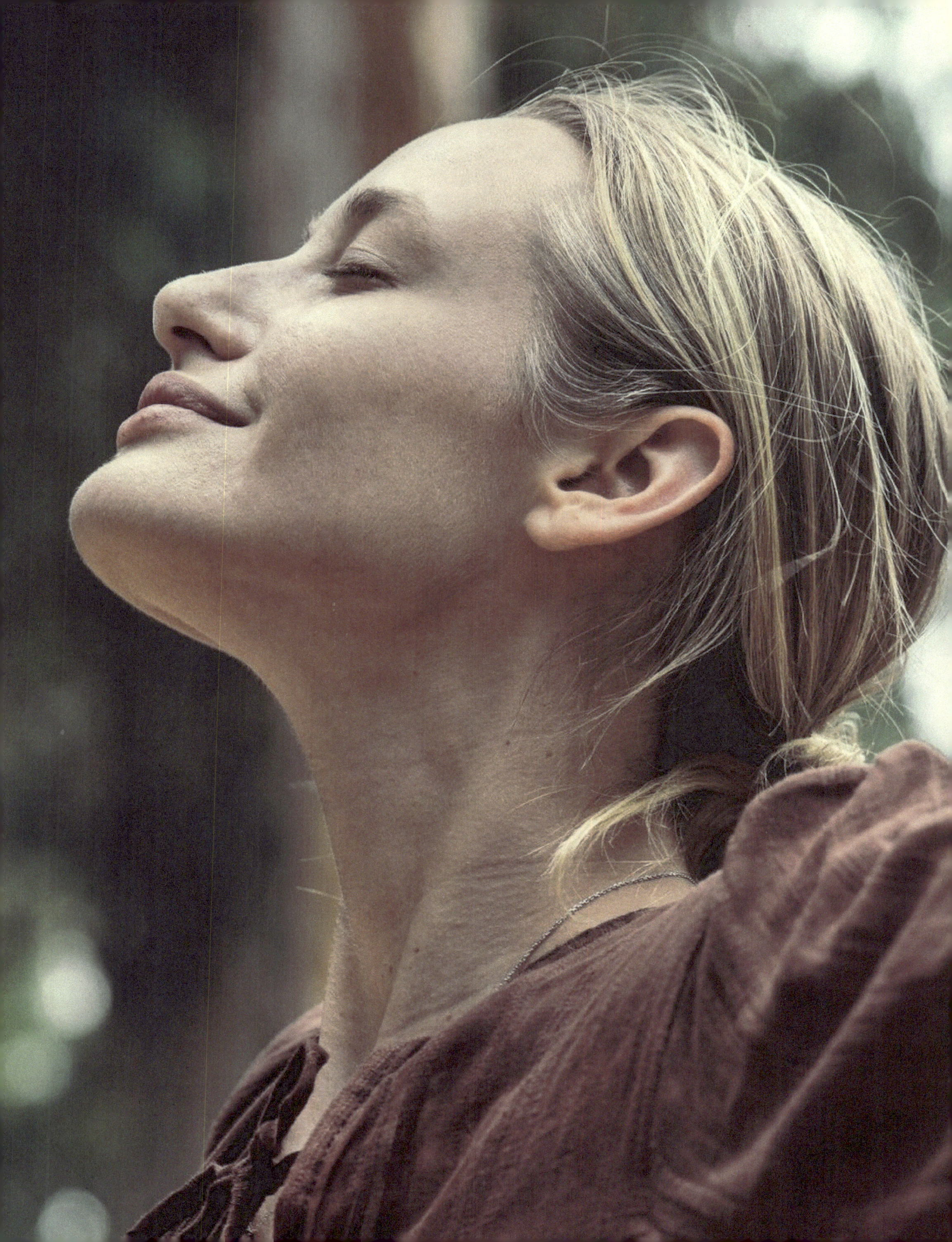

Freedom in New Covenant Expression

One of the first barriers many encounter in prophetic art is the inner critic—the voice that questions whether you are creative, spiritual, or skilled enough. In Christ, the old mindsets rooted in comparison, striving, and fear are broken. The New Covenant brings liberty to create without judgment or shame, because your identity is no longer tied to performance but to Jesus Himself.

Jesus, through His finished work, has removed every barrier between you and God—including barriers to your imagination and expression. Your hope rests in what He has already accomplished on the cross, not in your ability to "get it right." You are free to create as a response to grace, not as a means to earn approval. The judgments, critiques, and self-doubt dissolve as you align your mind with the truth of who you are: an empowered child of God, created for relationship, purpose, and beauty. His promise of abundant life means you have access to divine inspiration, freedom of expression, and joy in the creative process.

Freedom in New Covenant creativity means taking risks, embracing process over perfection, and finding delight in partnership with the Holy Spirit. It is an invitation to explore, to play, to discover the creativity God has woven into you without fear of falling short. When you exchange old mindsets for God's perspective, you step into a vibrant life where creativity flows naturally and confidently—an overflow of the abundance Christ has secured for you.

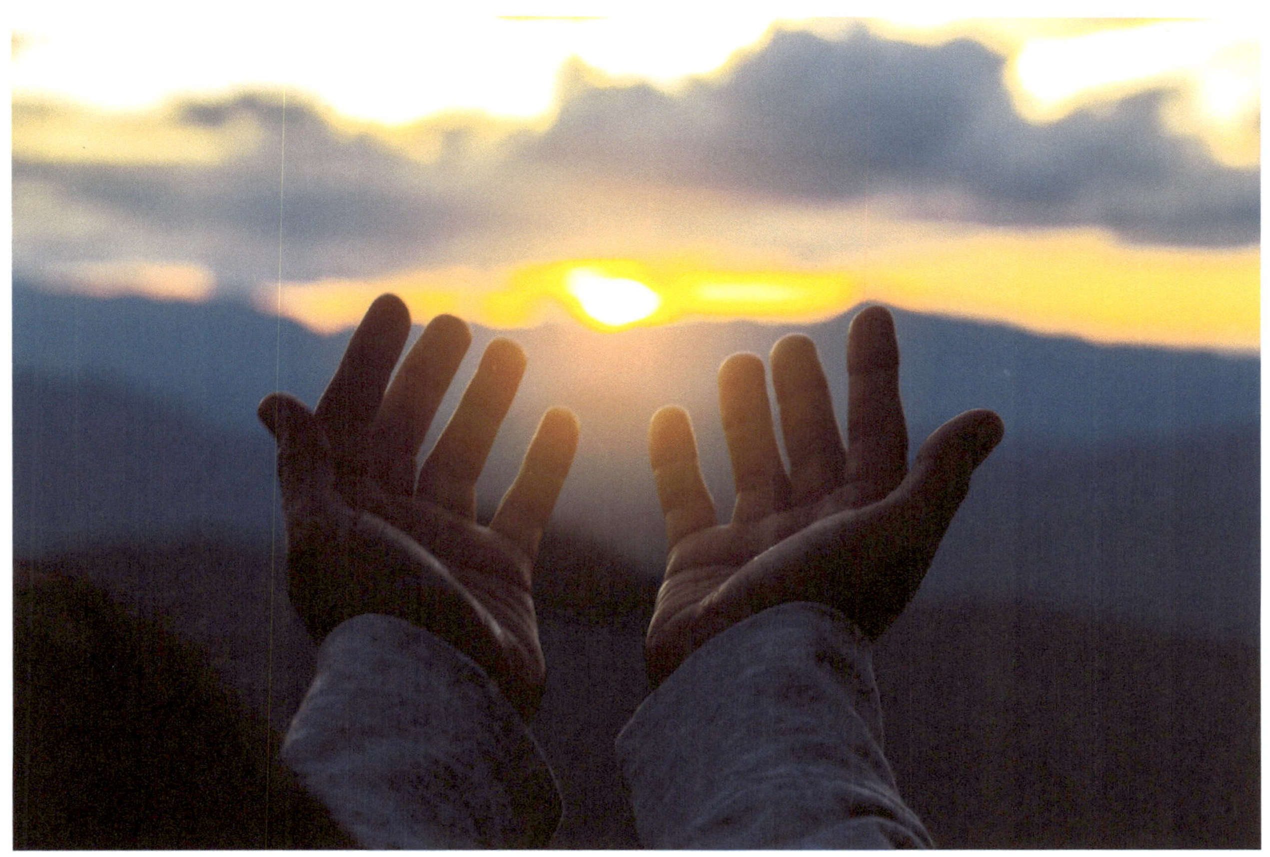

Renewing Your Mind

Transformation comes as we align our thoughts with God's truth. Take time to meditate on what He says about you as a creative being, and make it a daily practice to speak biblical affirmations aloud, letting His words saturate your mind and heart. These declarations anchor the truth of your New Covenant identity, reminding you who you are in Christ and reinforcing the freedom, authority, and creativity He has given you. Let His opinion become louder than your own doubts or the opinions of others, shaping not only your thinking but also the way you create, respond, and live each day.

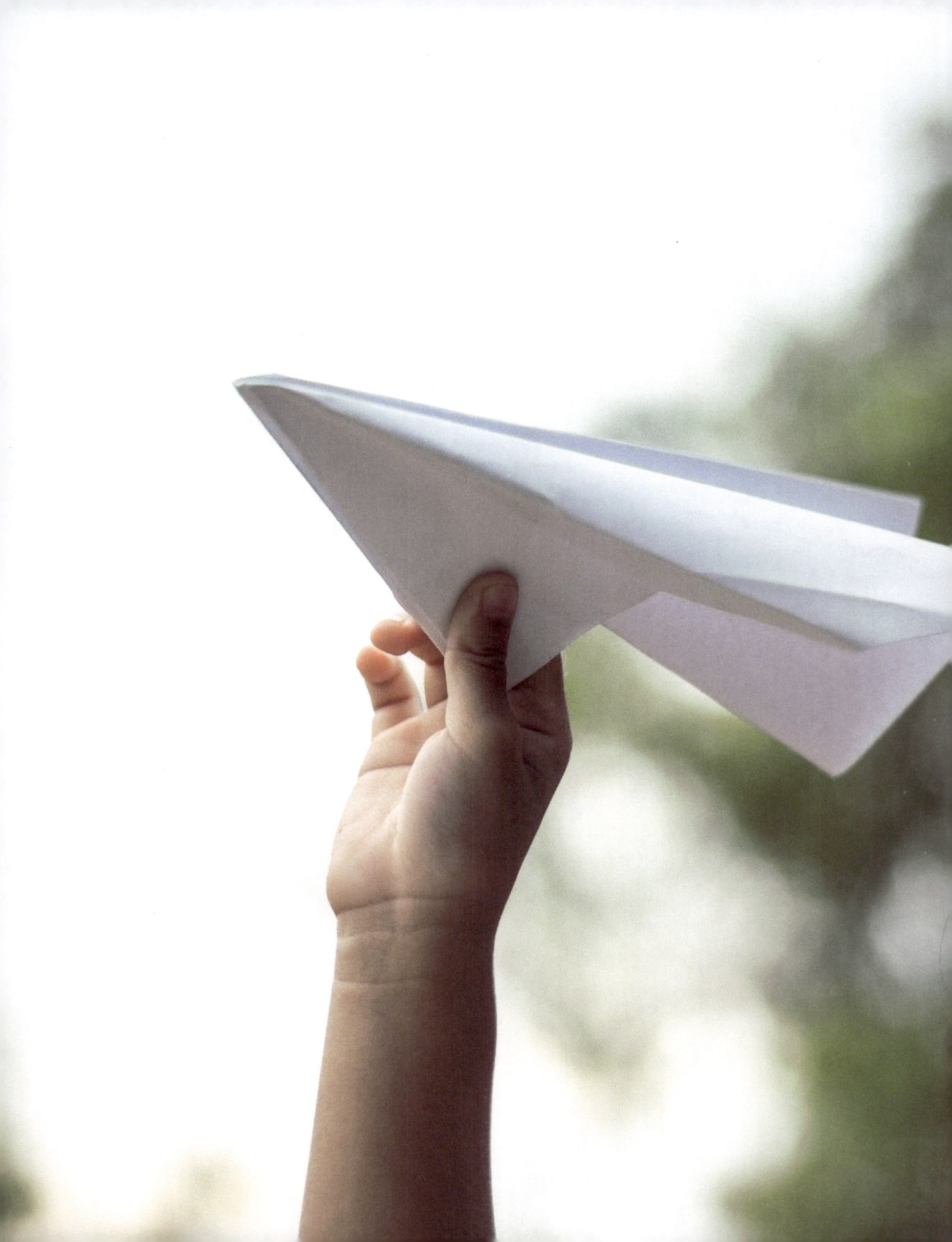

Childlike Freedom

"

Then Jesus called the children over to him and said to the disciples, "Let the little children come to me! Never send them away! For the Kingdom of God belongs to men who have hearts as trusting as these little children's. And anyone who doesn't have their kind of faith will never get within the Kingdom's gates."

Luke 18:16-17 (TLB)

Creativity flourishes when we approach art-making with the playfulness and curiosity of a child—free from the need to perform. The New Covenant restores this freedom, empowering you to create without fear of criticism or failure. Children live in an atmosphere of innocence; they are unburdened by the heaviness, shame, and self-consciousness that adulthood so often brings. In Christ, you have been restored to that same innocence—your New Covenant identity returns you to the purity Adam and Eve enjoyed before the fall, when they walked with God in Eden, the paradise of unhindered relationship. As you embrace this redeemed innocence, you create from a heart unburdened, open, and joyful, allowing prophetic art to flow naturally from the freedom and delight of simply being God's beloved child.

In prophetic art, childlike wonder becomes a doorway for the Holy Spirit to move, because a child's heart is open, unguarded, and responsive. As you let go of the pressure to be perfect and embrace the joy of exploration, you step into the same freedom Jesus celebrated when He said the Kingdom belongs to the childlike. This playful, trusting posture makes room for fresh inspiration, deeper intimacy, and a creativity that flows straight from the Father's heart.

My Prophetic Artist's Journey

My journey as a prophetic artist began with a surprising and life-altering prophetic word spoken over me by a seasoned prophet at a Prophetic Roundtable event. This man knew absolutely nothing about me—yet in just three minutes, he "read my mail" with stunning accuracy. Five times, the Lord emphasized that He wanted to release something new through me with art—something that would give expression to what I had walked through. Looking back, I believe the Lord was pointing to His healing work in my life, especially His restoration of my mind from the effects of diagnosed Post-Traumatic Stress Disorder. As He reestablished truth about my identity in Christ and the Kingdom of God within me, something deep inside was stirring.

At the time, I assumed the Lord was referring to my experience as a writer and graphic designer. I had decades of crafting, creating, and designing behind me, but no formal training in painting or illustration. Surely He meant my writing—something familiar. Yet I couldn't shake the sense that I needed to press further into this prophetic word.

Near the end of my 14 months at the School of the Prophets with Ivan Roman, God began leading me to two very different, Spirit-filled mentors in prophetic creativity: Matt Tommey and Theresa Dedmon. Through Matt, I learned about co-creating every part of life—and art—with God. Through Theresa, I discovered the vast, limitless ways prophetic art can heal, comfort, restore, deliver, and speak directly to the heart. Their teachings radically renewed my mind and expanded my understanding of how God moves through creative expression.

Transitioning from written words to visual language did not happen overnight. It felt like stepping onto a riverbank, hearing the sound of water, and wondering if I dared to wade in. The current of the Spirit was inviting but unfamiliar. The prophetic word functioned like a compass—steady, insistent, and alive. Each time I revisited it in prayer, I sensed fresh courage to risk, to explore, and to believe that the Lord's "new thing" could include materials, methods, and meanings I had never imagined.

Mentors, Mind Renewal, and the Call to Create

During this season, I began sensing that the prophetic word I received wasn't limited to writing at all. God was nudging me toward physical art—but what kind? What medium? As I prayed, I started having multiple prophetic dreams about creating paintings, including vibrant, colorful pieces connected to my ministry. Still, I didn't know what this would look like in the natural.

Matt always encouraged his students to step out, try new things, and explore the unique design God has woven into each of us. That encouragement became a catalyst. Theresa's testimonies about how art can comfort and deliver seemed to braid themselves with Matt's encouragement on co-creating with God in allignment with your unique design and purpose.

As these themes converged, I realized the Lord was inviting me to trust process over product. The point was not to produce a perfect canvas; it was to agree with Him in motion. Prophetic creativity, I learned, is listening with one's whole being—heart, mind, body, and spirit—and allowing that listening to shape color, composition, and flow. In that posture, the studio becomes a sanctuary, and the act of making becomes prayer.

The distance between imagination and obedience narrowed. I began to ask practical questions: What medium`s should I try first? How do I steward this hunger without forcing an outcome? In quiet, steady ways, the Lord kept saying, "Step forward—I'll meet you in the experiment." And so I did.

"

Jesus wants your mind infused, accessing unlimited wisdom and creativity, your body overflowing with supernatural energy.

Liz Wright

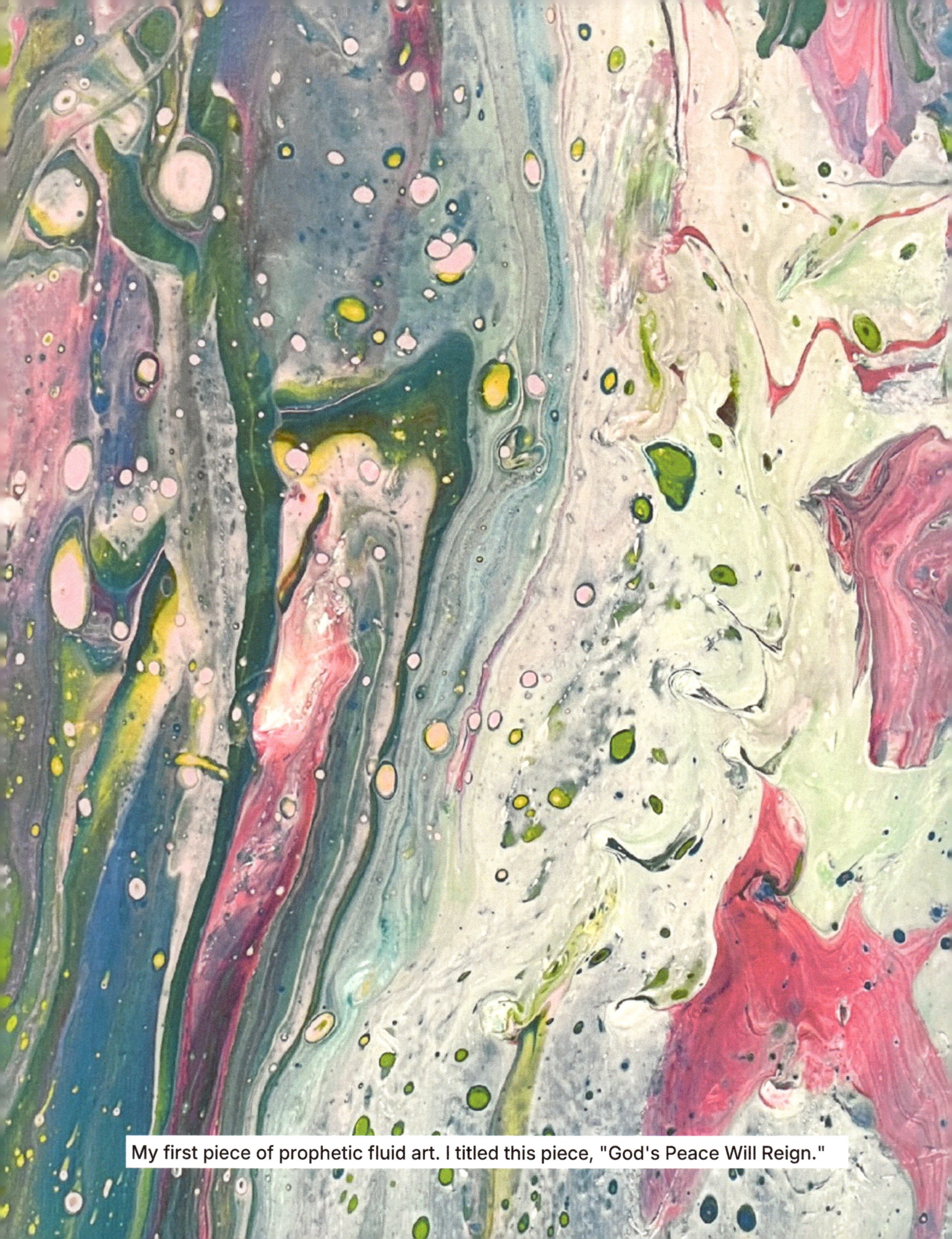

My first piece of prophetic fluid art. I titled this piece, "God's Peace Will Reign."

Discovering Fluid Art

Then, right as I was finishing Matt's course, my dear friend of twenty years, Vivien—a skilled portrait artist—felt the Holy Spirit nudge her to tell me about something called "pouring art," or Fluid Art. I had never heard of it. But once I began researching, watching tutorials, reading about it, and buying supplies, something inside me came alive. When I created my very first Fluid Art piece, it felt like a spark ignited. I knew instantly: This is it. I had found my artistic niche—something that fit my hands, my story, and my spirit.

Fluid Art felt like partnership in motion. The paint did not simply sit on the surface—it traveled, merged, divided, and revealed pathways I could not have planned. Tilt by tilt, swipe by swipe, cells opened like tiny windows, and color became its own vocabulary. My previous life in design gave me an eye for balance and contrast; my life in prayer taught me to wait and listen. In Fluid Art, both skills finally belonged to the same conversation.

I began to recognize how this medium mirrored my healing journey. Recovery from PTSD had not been a straight line; it came in waves, layers, and unexpected releases. In the same way, each pour carried a grace for unpredictability—a reminder that beauty can arise in the flow, not just after control. The canvas started to tell the truth: surrender is not passivity; it is responsive trust.

With each new piece, I sensed the Lord smiling over the process. He seemed to delight in teaching me how to notice subtle shifts—the viscosity of paint, the breath between movements, the patience to let things settle. In that noticing, worship became tactile, and color began to sing.

"

God conceals the revelation of his word in the hiding place of his glory. But the honor of kings is revealed by how they thouroughly search out the deeper meaning of all that God says.

Proverbs 25:2 (TPT)

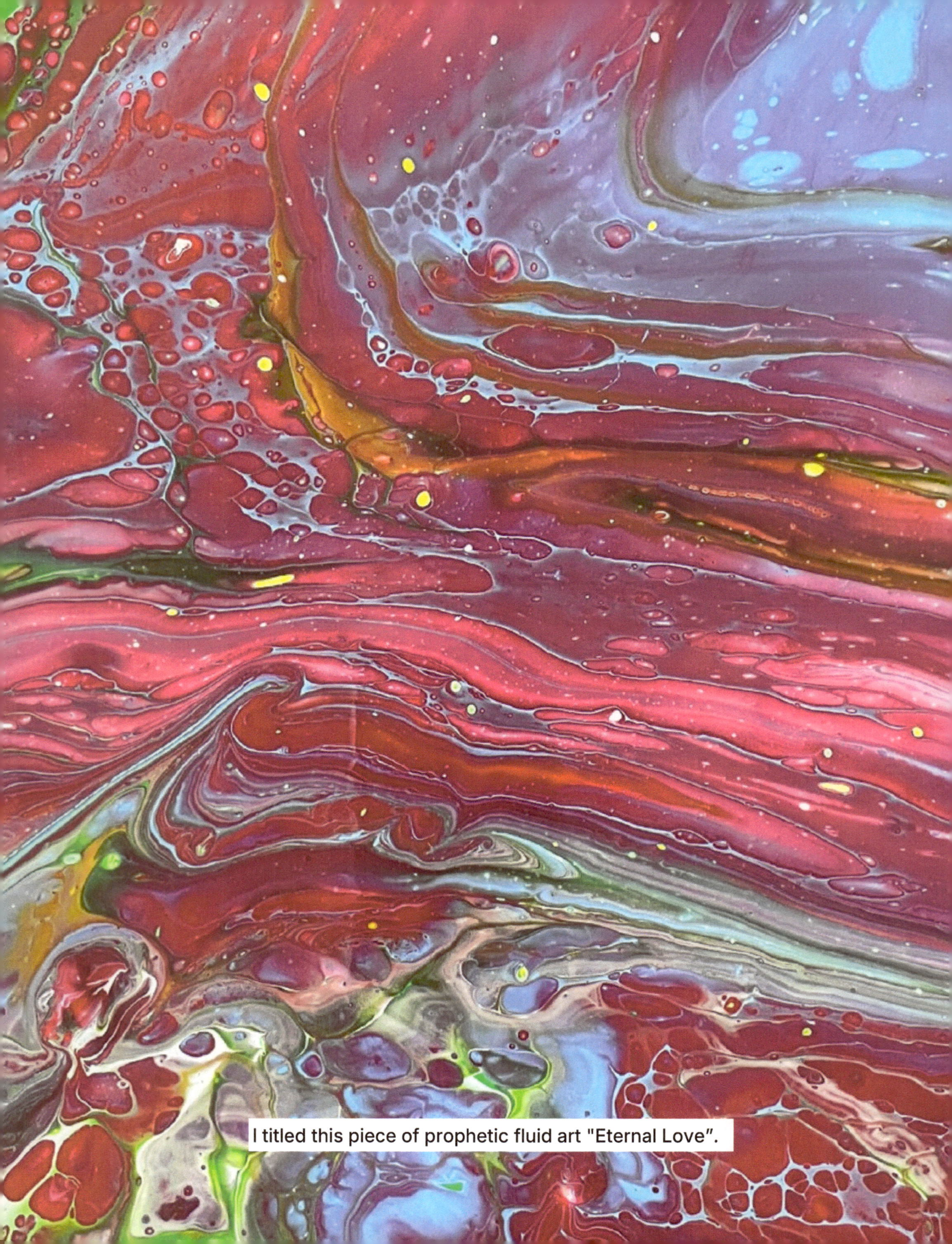

I titled this piece of prophetic fluid art "Eternal Love".

Diving Deep For Answers

Still, one question nagged at me: How could Fluid Art be prophetic? Everything I had seen labeled as prophetic art was representational—realistic images like the powerful painting Kirsty Pennington created, the very one God used to bring healing and identity back into my heart. So I took my questions to the Lord. And in His kindness, He began to expand my understanding.

Realistic prophetic art touches people because the imagery itself becomes a holy trigger—awakening memory, longing, identity, hope, and the promises in God's word. The image creates a landing place for the Holy Spirit to minister healing, guidance, and freedom. But God showed me that He wanted to release something new through me—something that didn't rely on a recognizable subject. He wanted to speak through color.

Colors can minister directly to the emotions. They can release peace, hope, courage, confidence, and healing—especially for those recovering from stress, depression, fear, and trauma - like the trauma I experienced during my 30+ years journey through PTSD.

This reframing felt both liberating and weighty. If color itself could be a vessel, then my stewardship of palettes, contrasts, and rhythms mattered deeply. Blues could cradle rest; golds could whisper worth; crimson could recall courage. The Spirit was composing through hue, and my task was to listen closely enough to choose well.

As I reflected on this revelation, I was reminded of the first day I attended one of Theresa Dedmon's live Zoom sessions. She released a prophetic word over me: "The Lord is calling you to heal the brokenhearted... like the pastel painting I did years ago of simply taking Jesus' hand, and how He shows you who you are in the midst of being thrown down, with no one there to lift you up. I'm telling you, your life is going to be a storyboard for **His glory to fall**—and you haven't seen anything yet." She knew nothing about my history with PTSD or that my ministry is called Glory Rain, yet her words struck the deepest chords of my story. Moments like that remind me how powerful prophetic words truly are—how they reveal our design, affirm our calling, and illuminate the purpose God has woven into our lives long before we ever see it for ourselves.

The Language of Color: Healing in Motion

Through Fluid Art, the Lord began to show me how colors can carry His presence, how nonrepresentational movement can bypass the analytical mind, and how prophetic expression doesn't always need a face or a figure to transform a heart. The canvas became a soft place to land for weary souls. My eyes rested on a gradient of blues and I breathed more deeply without knowing why.

In my own body, I noticed tenderness replacing tension as I created. The act of pouring demanded both attention and release—attention to mixture and timing, release to gravity and flow. That combination helped untangle old patterns of hypervigilance. When the paint moved, I learned to move with it. When it paused, I learned to wait.

I began to pray over palettes the way some pray over melodies. What color does peace want today? What shade will honesty wear? I found that certain combinations carried consistent meaning: white for purity and holiness; gold for glory and God's presence; purple hues for royalty and identity. The prophetic, in this context, was about presence—God's nearness braided into color and flow, and how His fingerprint uniquely marks each person who encounters the piece of art.

This is the new thing He has entrusted me with—prophetic art that speaks through color, movement, and the language of the Spirit. And it has become one of the most healing, joyful, and surprising parts of my walk with God.

Discover Your Unique Design

God has woven a unique design, purpose, and calling into your life, and prophetic art is one of the beautiful ways He reveals it. Just as He led me step by step—often through unexpected moments, gentle nudges, and prophetic confirmations—He will faithfully lead you into the fullness of who He created you to be. You don't have to force it or figure everything out on your own; the same Holy Spirit who awakened creativity in me will guide, teach, and equip you. As you lean into His voice and courageously follow His leading, you'll discover that every brushstroke, every idea, every act of creativity is part of your divine assignment. He has already prepared the path ahead, and He delights in empowering you to succeed in the very thing He designed you to do.

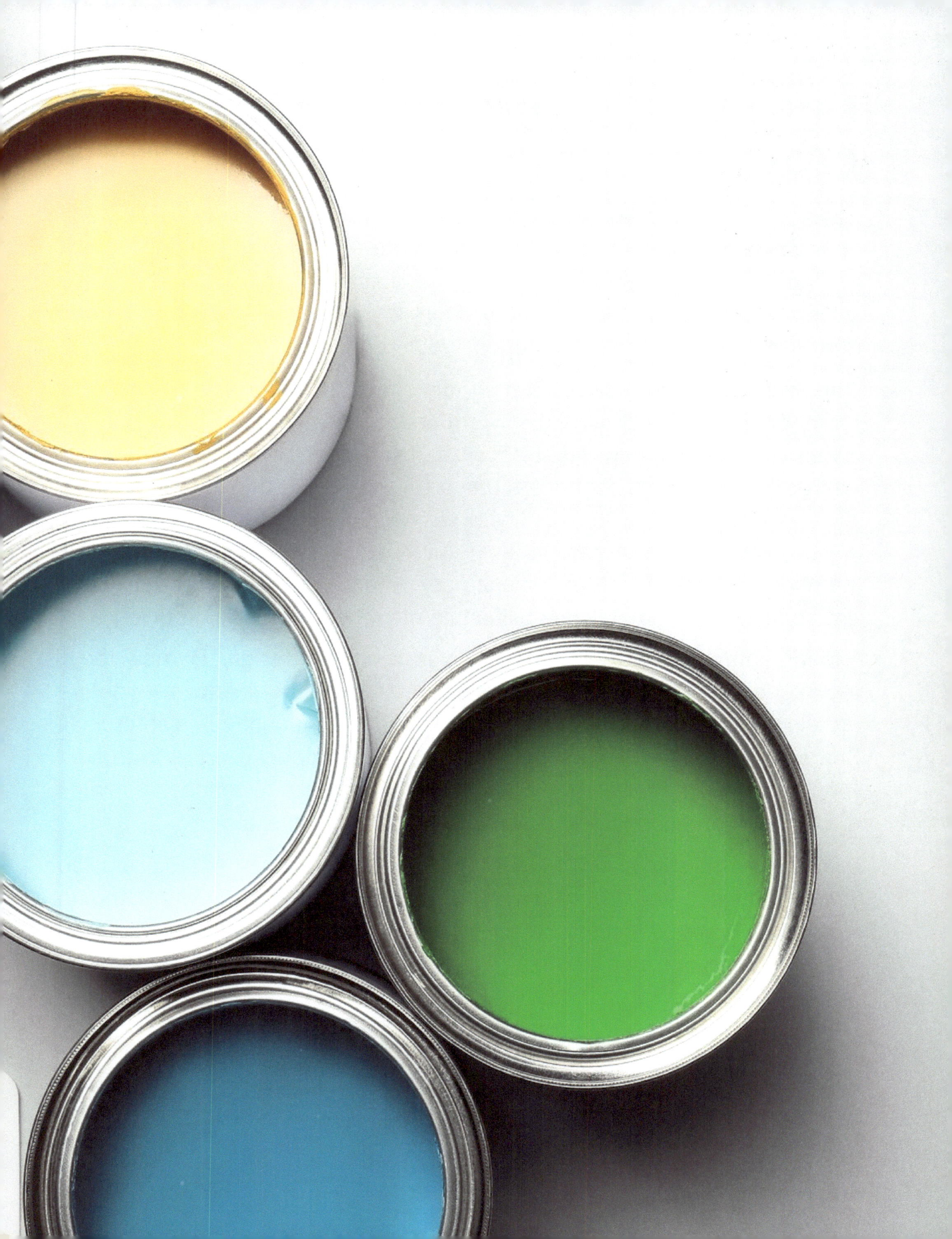

Developing Your Prophetic Art Practice

Developing a prophetic art practice involves both intentionality and spontaneity. Set aside regular times to create—whether in painting, music, writing, or another medium—inviting the Holy Spirit to lead. Make space for prayer, worship, and listening. Journaling God's impressions before, during, and after you create deepens your connection.

Consider setting up a designated studio space in your home—a corner, a room, or even a small table that you consecrate as a place of encounter. When you create a consistent physical environment where your materials are ready and the atmosphere is prayerful, your heart begins to recognize it as sacred ground. Surround yourself with things that stir your spirit: worship music, Scriptures, meaningful objects, or gentle lighting. This intentional space becomes a sanctuary where you can meet with God, dream with Him, and cultivate a lifestyle of creativity and communion.

Experimentation is vital in discovering your unique design. Try new tools, techniques, and styles. Don't be afraid to step into the unknown—you are growing in trust as you respond to inspiration. Community is also crucial. Share your creative process, testimonies, and prophetic art with trusted friends, worship leaders, or small groups. Openness invites encouragement, connection, and sometimes, new revelation.

Lastly, remember that prophetic art is about relationship. As you develop your practice, keep your focus on Him. Let your creativity become worship, communication, healing, and encouragement—a living demonstration of God's kindness on earth.

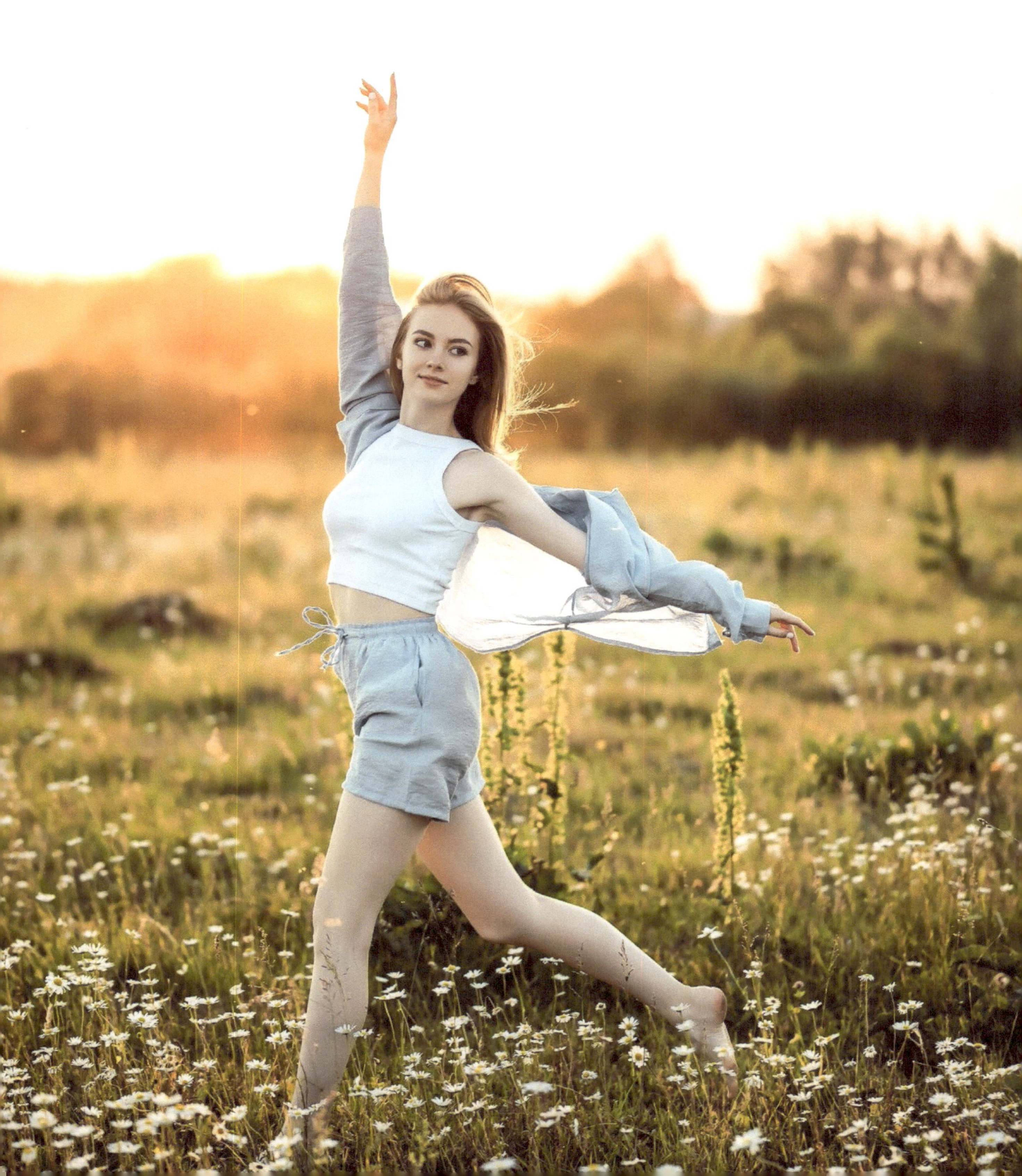

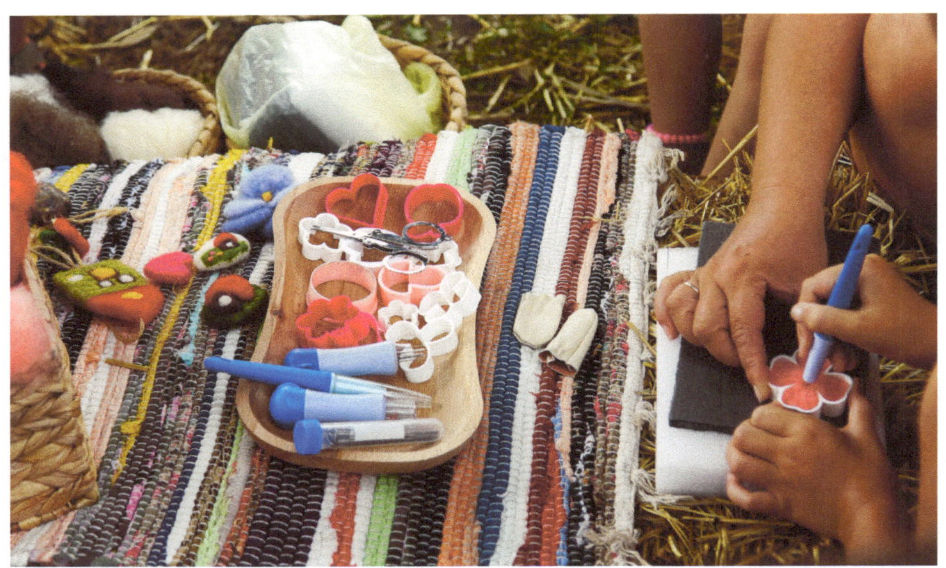

Practice With Purpose

Flow and excellence grow through regular practice with the Holy Spirit. Set time aside weekly to create with Him—even if it's just for a few minutes. Intentional practice builds confidence, skill, and faith for bigger creative assignments.

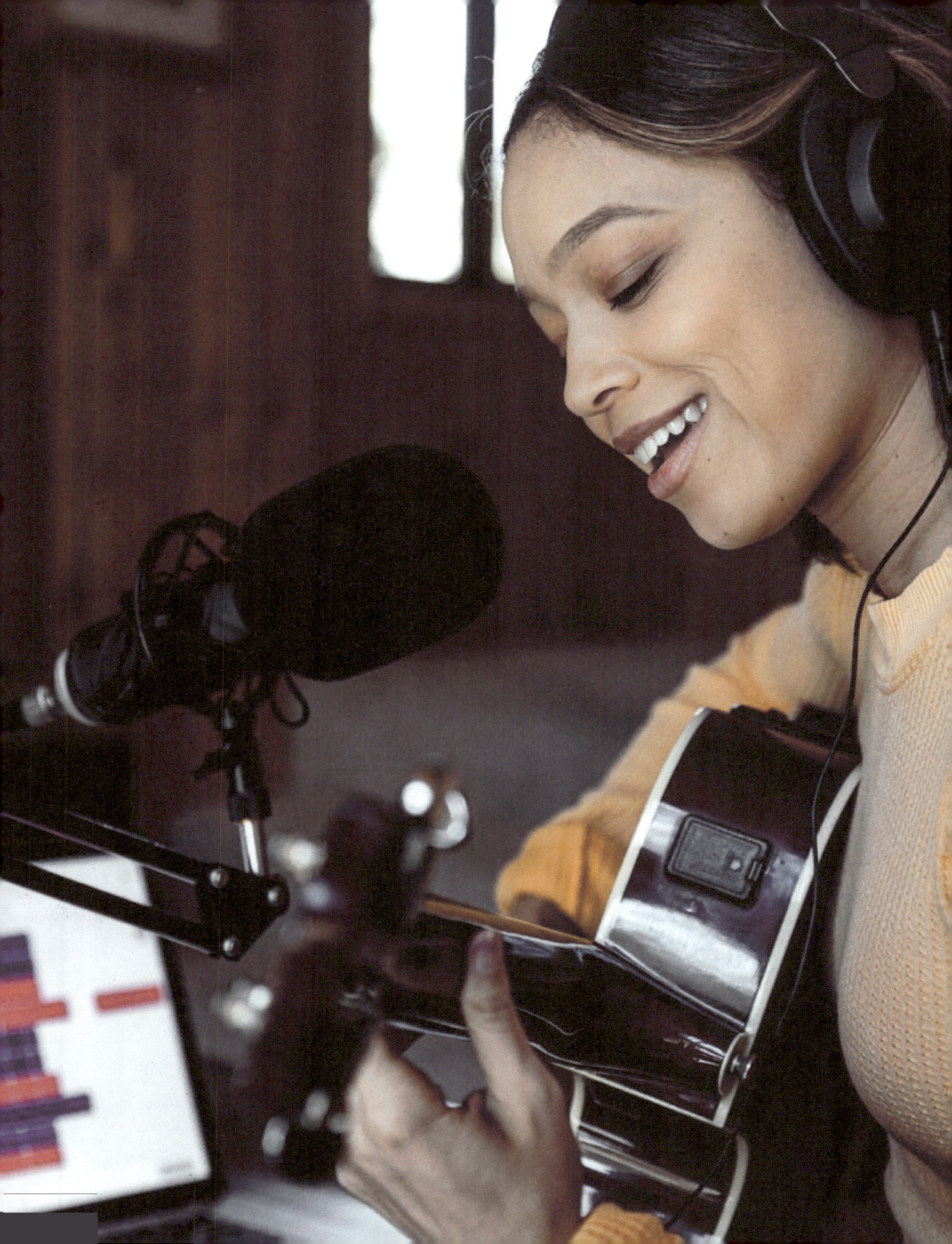

Share Your Journey

Don't hide your process. Sharing your experiences in safe community brings encouragement and often confirms what the Spirit is saying. Community also magnifies creativity—it's how God designed us to grow.

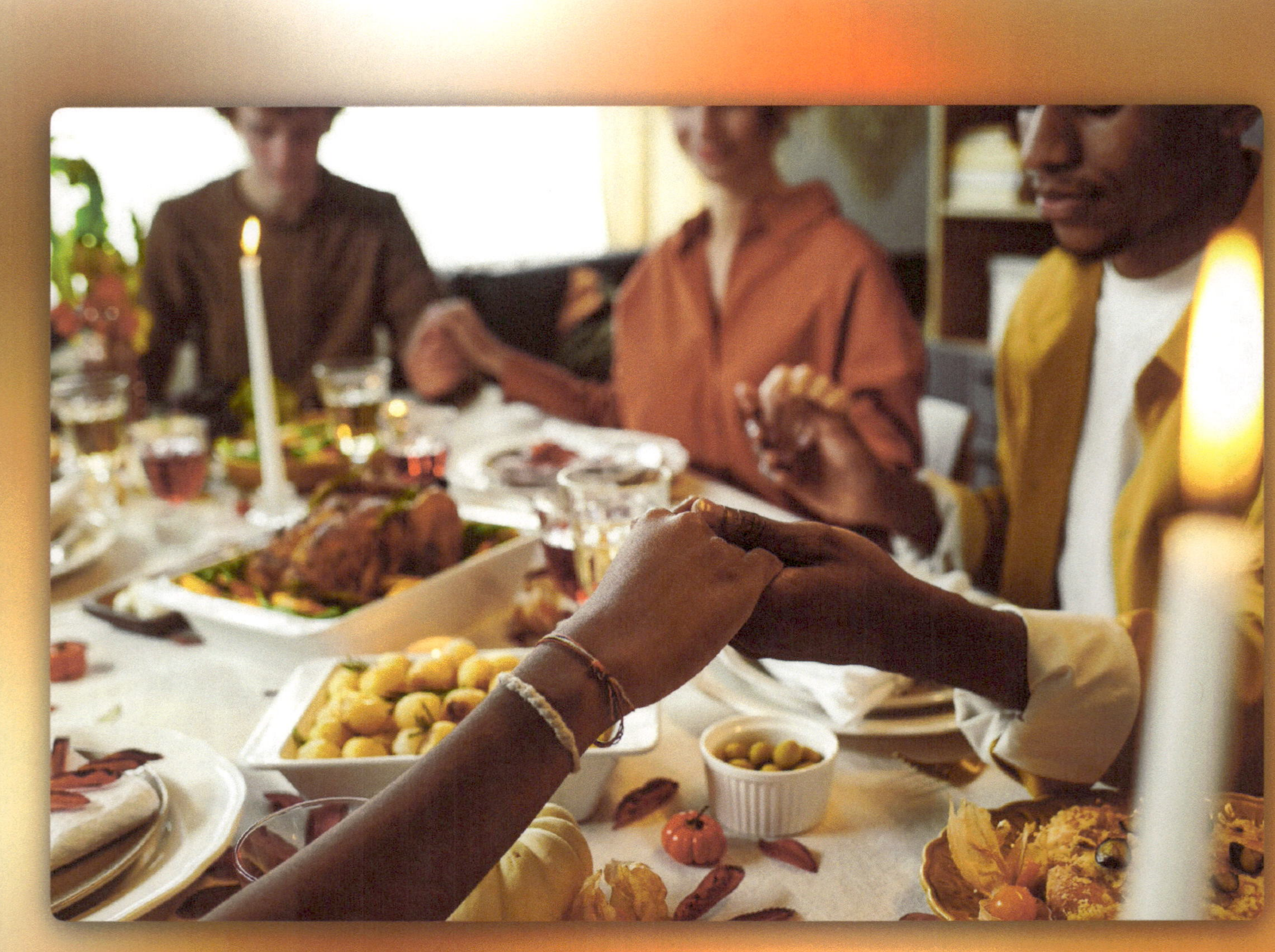

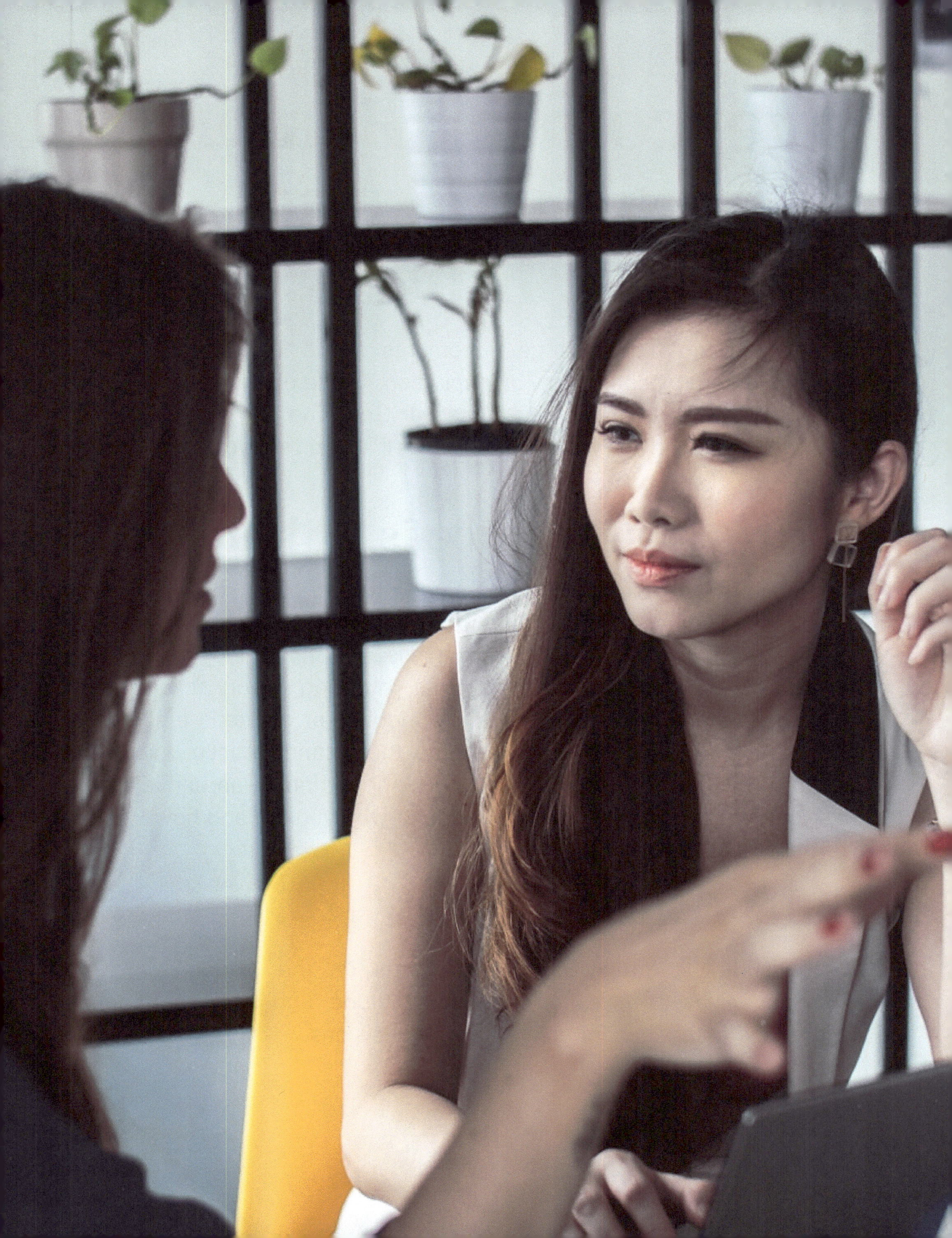

Overcoming Fear, Comparison, and Creative Blocks

Every creative faces challenges—moments where fear, comparison, or blocks threaten to halt the flow of inspiration. These obstacles often come from old wounds or lies about yourself or God. The good news: perfect love casts out fear. As you ground yourself in God's love, fear loses its hold.

Your Artistic Voice is Unique

Comparison is another trap, convincing you that your creativity is less valuable than someone else's. The Holy Spirit reminds you that your voice, style, and story are unique and necessary. The world needs your perspective—no one else can offer what you bring in your unique voice and style. Others may work in a similar medium or create in a style that looks familiar, but no one can replicate the distinct artistic voice God placed within you. It is as singular as your fingerprints—an unmistakable mark of identity that carries the essence of who you are and how Heaven expresses itself through you.

Quiet Confidence

Comparison kills creativity. instead, focus on the unique way God expresses Himself through you. Let gratitude and quiet confidence become the foundation for your creativite decisions.

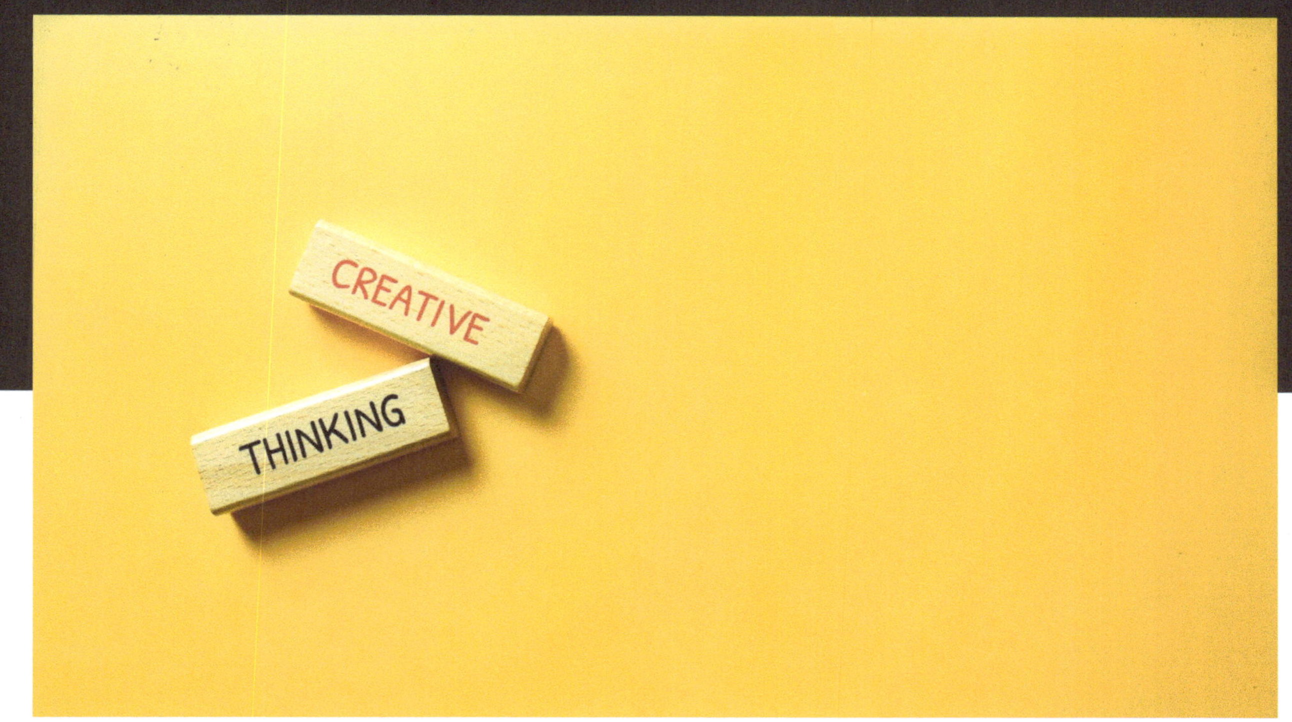
CREATIVE
THINKING

Breaking Through Blockages

Invite the Holy Spirit into moments of block. Sometimes breakthrough comes through rest, play, or shifting focus from performance to presence. Trust that God is always for you, even when you don't feel inspired.

Creative blocks are not a sign to give up. Sometimes, they are invitations to rest, to change direction, or to press deeper into God's presence. Be open to the possibility that God may be leading you in a direction you didn't anticipate—one that ultimately proves far better than anything you could have imagined. In those unexpected pivots, having a supportive, faith-filled creative community becomes essential. Cultivate gratitude, take walks in nature, worship, and remember to ask for fresh inspiration. What seems like a block is often the beginning of a new breakthrough.

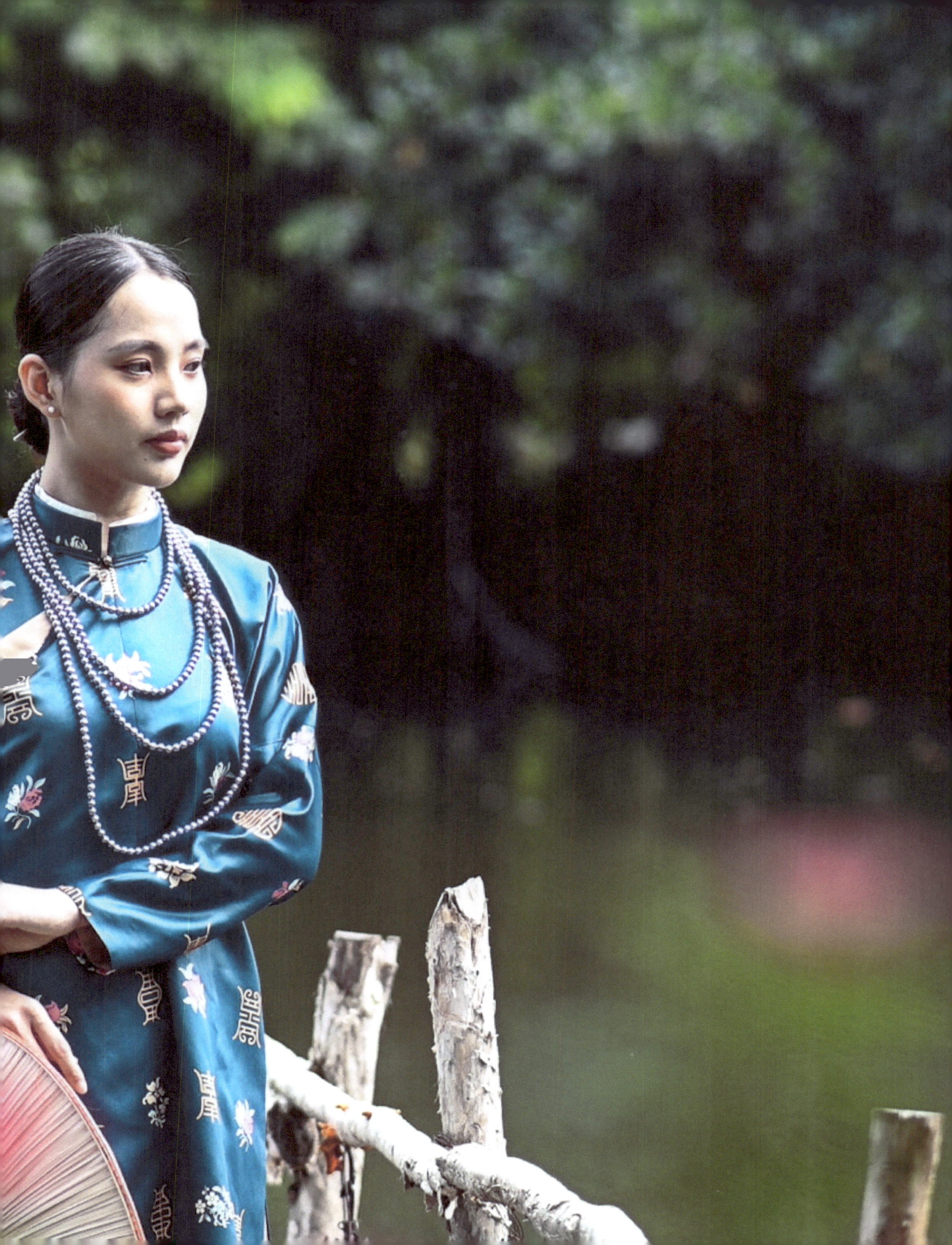

Healing and Hope

Personal testimonies abound of breakthrough and healing through prophetic paintings, music, and poetry. In God's hands, creativity becomes a key for unlocking hearts and bringing hope to the hopeless. Prophetic art is truly transformational—many who create or receive it encounter deep healing, fresh hope, and renewed vision for their lives. When art is birthed under the leadership of the Holy Spirit, it ministers directly to the heart, dismantling lies, releasing truth, and offering encouragement for the journey ahead.

Restored Identity

One of the key roles of prophetic art is to restore identity—reminding us who we are as children of God living a fully redeemed life under the New Covenant. Through these Spirit-breathed expressions, we are invited to step into the reality that the fullness of God's Kingdom, with all its abundance and shalom—wholeness in spirit, soul, and body—belongs to us and is accessible now, today. The Tree of Life and the River of Life flow from within you through the Holy Spirit, and prophetic art becomes one of the beautiful ways God releases that river, awakening identity, renewing hope, and restoring the divine life He placed inside you, and the people you are ministering to.

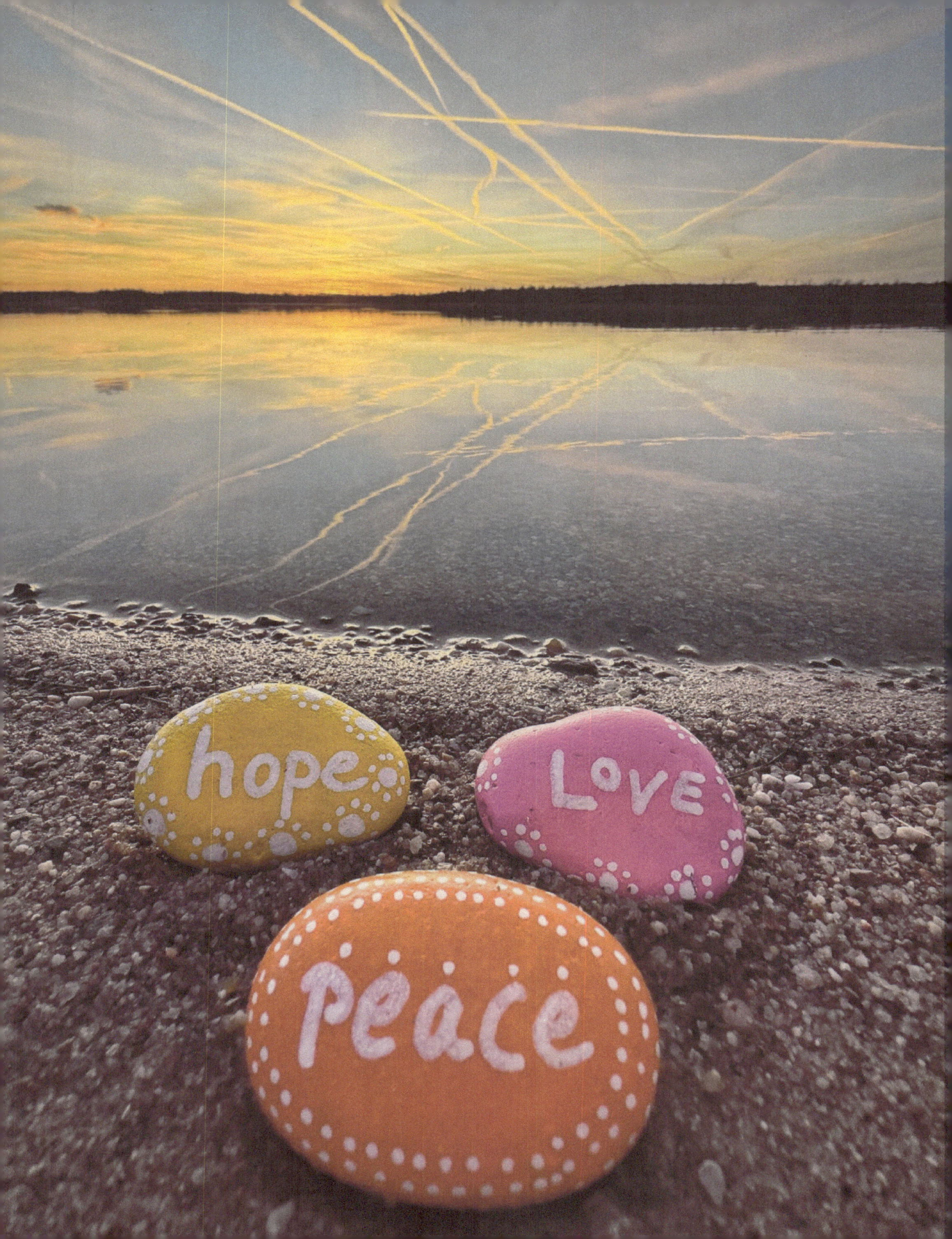
hope
Love
peace

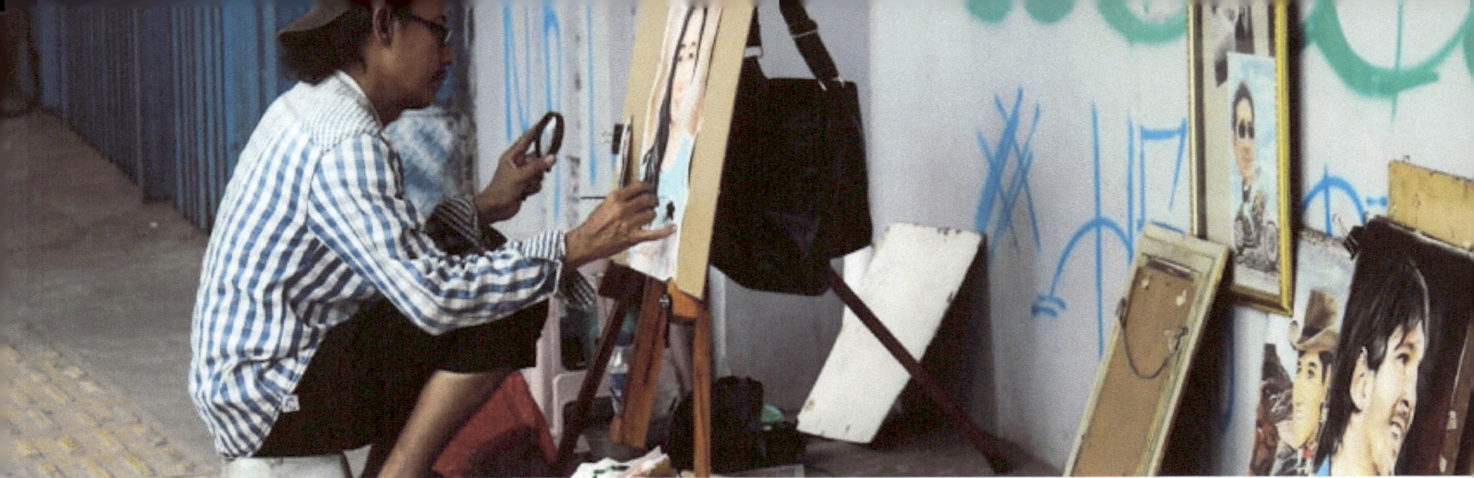

Revival in Community

“

The prophetic Scriptures also conclude, that the proclaiming of this message, celebrating the authority and meaning of his name, will inevitably lead to a co-knowing, a joint awakening, engaging the full realization of the complete remission of sins. What has happening here in Jerusalem, will continue to circle out like ripples becoming unstoppaable tsunami wave, overwhelming the mass of humanity. The royal reign of the good news of their redeemed identity and innocence is the context of this proclamation.

Luke 24 47 (THE MIRROR)

Within communities, prophetic art can shift atmospheres, unite people in purpose, and awaken hearts to God's presence. Murals painted during worship, prophetic poems spoken over a congregation, or original songs released in response to a word—all of these open doors for spiritual renewal and deep connection. Prophetic art ushers in fresh revival, becoming a catalyst for spiritual awakening as the Holy Spirit moves through creative expression, drawing people into powerful encounters with God and with one another.

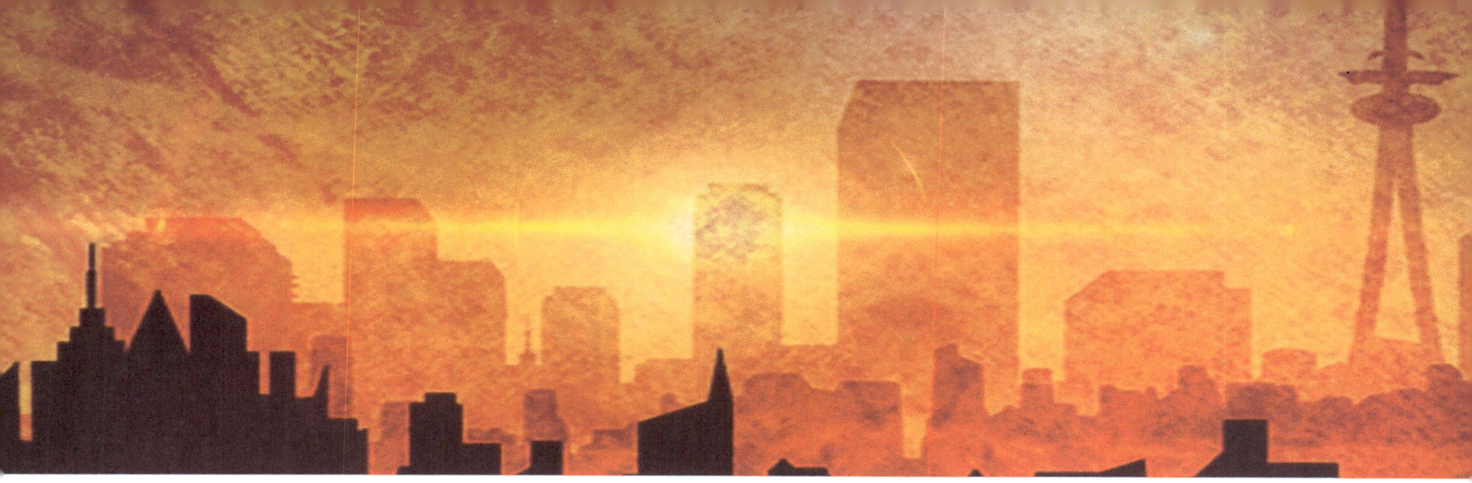

Kingdom Outreach

Transformation does not stop at the church door. Many artists find their creative expression opening doors into schools, hospitals, and neighborhoods—bringing beauty, hope, and miracles into places that need God's love most. Your art becomes a powerful tool for outreach; whether it appears in a gallery, a street mural, or online, God will use your creativity to carry His message—and His transformative power—farther than you can imagine. When your art is released in faith and rooted in love, its impact is multiplied, touching hearts and shifting atmospheres in ways only Heaven can orchestrate.

Growing Your Vision

As a prophetic artist, don't hesitate to ask God for a breaker anointing—an anointing that empowers you to boldly expand your artistic voice into new territory. The Holy Spirit delights in leading you beyond your comfort zone and into fresh realms of expression where Heaven's creativity flows unhindered. When you partner with Him, fear loses its grip, limitations crumble, and the boundaries around your creativity begin to stretch in miraculous ways. Trust that God is not only enlarging your artistic capacity but also giving you the courage to step into places you've never gone before, carrying His presence and His message with confidence and authority.

Conclusion: Creativity and Co-Creating With God

Prophetic art is an invitation to live a life bigger, freer, and more beautiful than you ever imagined. God did not create you to be a spectator, but a creative partner. Every day offers new opportunities to receive His inspiration and respond in love. But prophetic art doesn't just happen—you must be intentional. You have to say yes to God, lean into His leading, and follow the Holy Spirit toward the vision He has planted within you. Remember that prophetic creativity flows from the overflow of your intimacy with God; what you create on the outside is born from the communion you cultivate on the inside. As you continue this journey, remember that creativity is not about competition or perfection. It's about connection—with God, with people, and with the world that hungers for hope and transformation.

Let your life be God's canvas and your creativity His brush. Dream boldly. Create fearlessly. Release beauty freely as a living testimony of Heaven touching earth. Live every day—100% led by the Holy Spirit—partnering in the radical good news of the New Covenant.

Now the invitation is yours—step in, create, and never look back. The world is waiting for what God and you will make together.

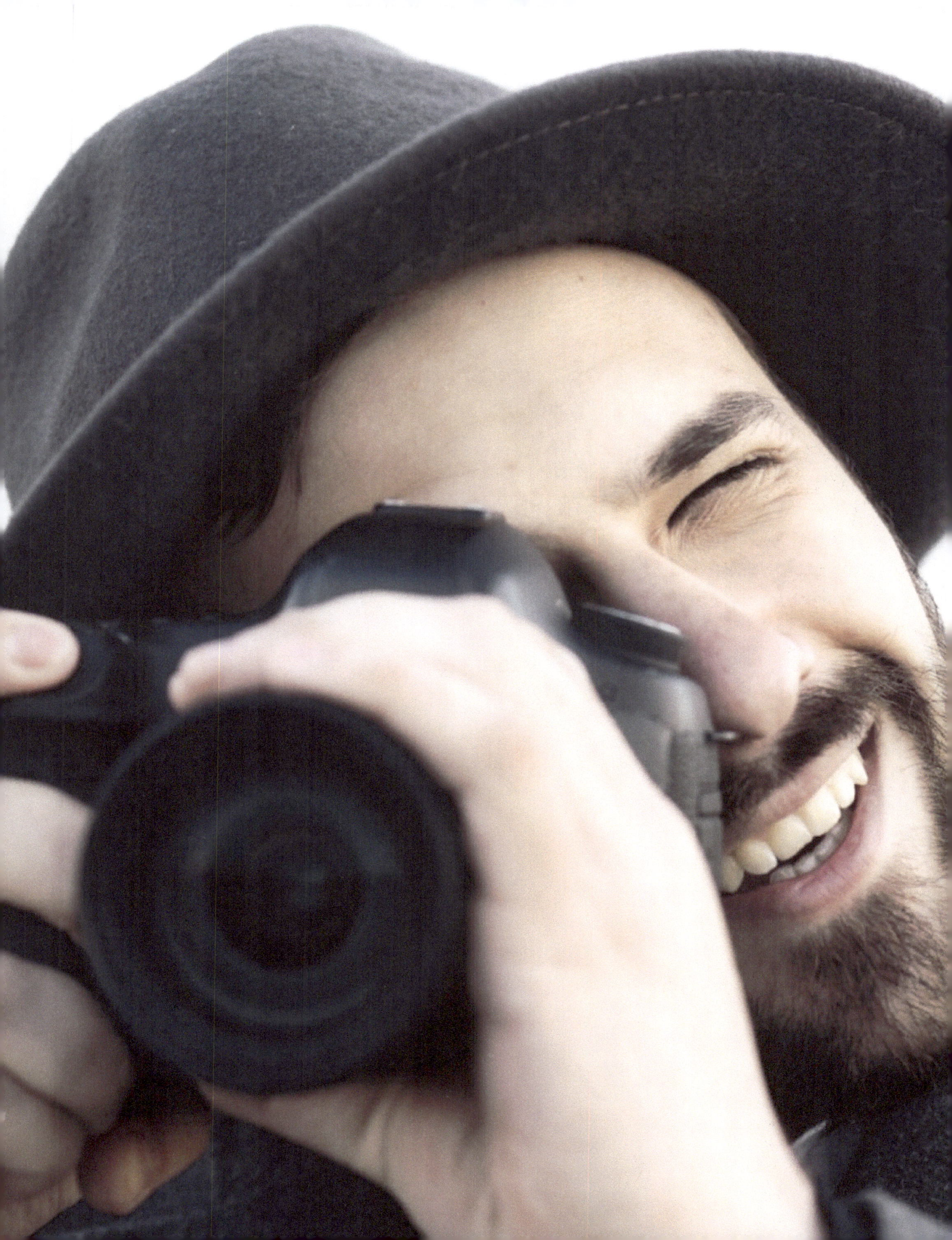

CHAPTER NOTES

Banov, Georgian
Joy: God's Secret Weapon For Every Believer (Grand Rapids, MI: Chosen Books, 2021, pg. 138).

Dedmon, Theresa *Born To Create: Stepping Into Yout Supernatural Destiny (*Shippensburg, PA: Destiny Image Publishers, Inc., 2012, pg. 23).

Toit, Francois du *Mirror Study Bible:The Romance of the Ages* (www.mirrorword.net, 2025, pg. 27).

Tommey, Matt *Prophetic Art: A Practical Guide To Creating With The Holy Spirit* (www.MattTommeyMentoring.com, 2021, pg. 15).

Wright, Liz *Reflecting God: Spiritual Keys To Unlock The Supernatural You* (Liz Wright Ministries Ltd., 2020, pg. 24).

Invitation to Join Our Private Community

Are you a prophetic artist who longs to create with God—not just for Him?

Do you desire a safe, Spirit-led space where creativity, worship, and revelation flow together?

You're invited to join my private Facebook group,

Prophetic Art: Creativity & Co-Creating With God

This is a nurturing community for artists, creatives, and visionaries who want to:

- Grow in hearing God's voice through art
- Explore creativity as both intimacy and spiritual expression
- Share artwork, processes, and testimonies in a grace-filled environment
- Be encouraged, equipped, and inspired by fellow prophetic artists
- Co-create with the Holy Spirit in freedom, joy, and confidence

Whether you paint, draw, write, journal, create digitally, dance, photograph, ect., or are just beginning to explore prophetic creativity—there is a place for you here.

Come as you are.

Create from rest.

Partner with God.

Request to join Prophetic Art: Creativity & Co-Creating With God

I would love to welcome you into this growing, Spirit-led community.

About Lynne Valle

Lynne Valle is a prophetic fluid artist and creative minister whose life and work flow from one passion: revealing the beauty, freedom, and intimacy of life in Christ. Her art is birthed in worship, prayer, and deep listening—each piece a visual expression of God's heart, filled with prophetic meaning, New Covenant identity, and the transformative love of Jesus.

After raising her large family, Lynne experienced a life-changing visitation from the Lord that awakened her to vivid spiritual dreams, encounters, and prophetic words from trusted leaders. These moments ignited her calling into prophetic ministry and opened a new chapter of creative partnership with the Holy Spirit.

Her journey of equipping includes training with the School of the Prophets under Ivan Roman, the International Prophetic Movement, the Global Celebration Supernatural School of Ministry, the Kingdom Creative Movement with Theresa Dedmon, the Created to Thrive Foundation Course with Matt Tommey, and Emerging Apostles with Ian Carroll. These experiences strengthened her understanding of the prophetic, creativity, and the abundant life Jesus promised in John 10:10.

Today, Lynne ministers both locally and globally—through her blog, online communities, prophetic art, teaching, and in-person gatherings. She carries a joyful conviction that every believer has full access to intimacy with God and the Tree of Life right now, and she loves helping people step into their God-given identity as image-bearers and co-creators with Him.

Her prophetic fluid art holds a special place in her ministry. Through color, movement, symbolism, and Spirit-led flow, Lynne creates pieces that release healing, peace, identity, and the tangible presence of God. Each painting becomes a prophetic encounter—inviting others to experience God's voice, beauty, and affection in fresh, deeply personal ways.

A Life Rooted in Faith, Family, and Creativity

Raised in the vibrant suburbs of New York City as a second-generation American, Lynne's journey is woven with threads of faith, resilience, and creativity. She is a devoted mother of eight (including one daughter now with Jesus) and a joyful grandmother, gracefully balancing family life with her work as an artist, graphic designer, writer, and minister.

Through every season of her life, Lynne's passion remains the same: to bring glory to God by creating beauty, releasing hope, and helping others discover the abundant, intimate, Spirit-filled life they were designed for.

Stay Connected

Digital Products Website:
lynnevalle.shop

YouTube

Facebook

Instagram

Gloroy Rain Website:
gloryrain.store

Picture Books Website:
lynnevalle.com

Grab Your FREE Copy of My eBook:

Creative Prayed For: Prophetic Artists — Embracing Your New Covenant Identity **is an invitation into a life-giving way of connecting with God through creativity, prayer, and identity.**

Written for artists and creatives of all kinds—painters, writers, dancers, musicians, designers, and more—this ebook gently opens the door to hearing God's voice in the freedom and assurance of the New Covenant. Whether you are just beginning to explore prophetic art or have been creating with God for years, this book meets you where you are and encourages growth without pressure or performance.

Inside, you'll discover 30 creative prayer prompts designed as prayerful expressions through action. These are not prayers you simply read, but experiences you enter—inviting the Holy Spirit to move through your hands, imagination, and creative process. Each prompt creates space to listen, respond, and co-create with God in a way that feels natural, joyful, and deeply personal.

The book also shares the author's personal testimony of transformation and breakthrough, along with clear, hope-filled teachings on:

- **Creative prayer as a relational practice**
- **New Covenant identity for prophetic artists and creatives**
- **Creating from rest, grace, and belovedness—not striving**
- **Growing in confidence as you hear and respond to God's voice**

Creative Prayed For is not about getting it "right," but about discovering the freedom to create with God from who you already are in Christ. It's an encouragement to explore, to trust, and to embrace creativity as a sacred space where prayer becomes art—and art becomes prayer.

Perfect for individuals, small groups, or creative prayer times, this ebook offers a fresh, grace-centered approach to prophetic creativity that empowers you to grow, listen, and create in partnership with God—right where you are today.

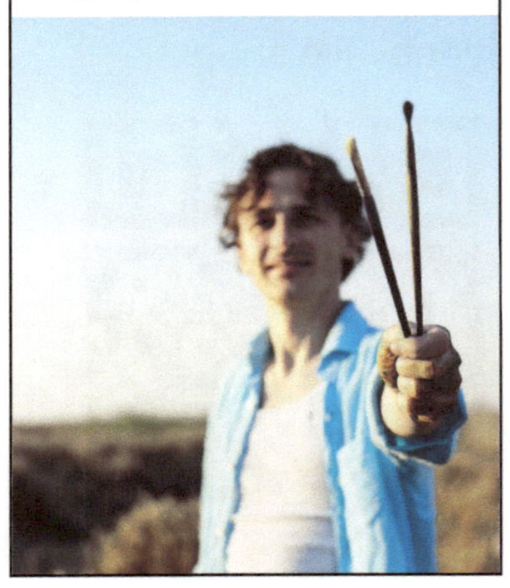

Use the QR code to receive the FREE ebook Creative *Prayer for Prophetic Artists* — including 30 printable creative prayer prompts.

NOTE: This QR code goes to the sign up page on my digital products shop - lynnevalle.shop

Please Write A Review

Thank you for spending your valuable time reading *Prophetic Art: Creativity & Co-Creating With God.* If this blessed, encouraged, or inspired you in any way, I would be so grateful if you would take a moment to share your thoughts in a review.

Your review is, in essence, your testimony—and testimonies have power. They help spread this message of God's radical grace and abundant life to others who are searching for hope. Every review makes a difference and is an encouragement not only to me but to many future readers.

Thank you for partnering with me to get this message out to the world!

www.ingramcontent.com/pod-product-compliance
Lightning Source LLC
LaVergne TN
LVHW070146110826
845147LV00002B/335
9798999206855